John Hopkins was a writer who, after graduating from Princeton, lived for many years in Tangier and was a central figure in the bohemian literary crowd of the '60s and '70s, becoming friends with William Burroughs, Paul Bowles and Jane Bowles. He wrote several novels, among them *Tangier Buzzless Flies* and *The Flight of the Pelican*, and travel memoirs including *The Tangier Diaries* and *The South American Diaries*.

THE WHITE NILE DIARIES

JOHN HOPKINS

TP

TAURIS PARKE
Bloomsbury Publishing Plc
50 Bedford Square, London, WC1B 3DP, UK
29 Earlsfort Terrace, Dublin 2, Ireland

BLOOMSBURY, TAURIS PARKE and the TAURIS PARKE logo are
trademarks of Bloomsbury Publishing Plc

First published in 2014
This edition published in 2021

A catalogue record for this book is available from the British Library
Library of Congress Cataloguing-in-Publication data has been
applied for

ISBN: 978-0-7556-4745-3
eISBN: 978-0-85773-484-6

Inside map: *The Voyage of the White Nile made by John Hopkins and
Joe McPhillips (July–October 1961)*. Map drawn by Lawrence Mynott

Dedicated to the memory of Joe McPhillips

* * *

Impala Farm
P.O. Box 92, Nanyuki
Kenya Colony
British East Africa
January 4, 1961

TO:
The Undergraduate Secretary
The Ivy Club
Prospect St.
Princeton University
Princeton, N.J.
U.S.A.

Sir,

The American Consulate out here has asked all resident Americans to rally around, and do something about the university students from the States who arrive here on their holidays with no contacts, and want to see the country, do some shooting, exploring, mountain climbing, etc., and need a base that wouldn't use up their spare cash!

As I'm Princeton and Ivy '40, thought I would let charity begin at home, and drop you a line, and say that I would be delighted to have anyone from the Vine make this their headquarters and stay as long as they like.

This is a 46,000-acre cattle ranch – low veldt – on the equator right beside the snows of Mount Kenya, 16,000 feet high, with the Northern Frontier District and then Abyssinia on the East and North. There is lots of game – elephant – rhino – lion – leopard – hippo – cheetah – giraffe – eland – oryx and all the lesser buck and very good bird shooting. Mt. Kenya is interesting to climb and the game parks in the N.F.D. are excellent.

The native situation is still in hand here except for constant cattle raiding, and this district is as safe as any place in Africa, *at the moment*, but scarcely carte blanche. We are all well forted up, and armed, and ready to ride out the coming storm. Not trying to scare anyone off but it's no country to go bicycling or hitch-hiking.

If anyone is interested and coming out, get them to contact me, and I'd be delighted to do what I could. I'm sure the Club is flourishing as always.

Yours sincerely,

Sam Small '40

P.S. There are quite a few temp. ranch jobs open at this time of year – not necessarily on horseback and not very comfortable if anyone would want that.

S.S.

*   *   *

It all began at the Oyster Bar in Grand Central Station in New York.

I was sitting at the counter with Kevin Madden filling up on cherrystones and bluefish. Kevin and I were classmates, clubmates, and good friends from Princeton. He was our class secretary at the Ivy Club.

I had just returned from half a year in South America with Joe McPhillips and Harry Rulon-Miller, investigating our romantic ambition of buying a coffee plantation in the Peruvian jungle. We had had many adventures but, in the end, the dream evaporated. There was already too much coffee in the world. To keep the price up, Brazil was throwing half its crop into the sea. The planters we met were colorful characters, but all up to their ears in debt to the banks. Harry had to head home early. In a park in Yurimaguas (Loreto Province), with the parrots screaming above our heads, Joe and I finally concluded that, at the ages of 22 and 24, we were not prepared to spend the next 25 years of our lives in the jungle.

Neither did we want to return to the U.S. with our tails between our legs, face family pressure to settle down, get jobs (and get married). After sliding down the Upper Amazon on a balsa raft, the fire for adventure was still burning in our veins. In that bar we mapped out a provisional plan to pursue our travels in Europe. The first thing we did when we got back to New York was to book passage on the *Saturnia*, an ancient vessel headed on her final voyage to Italy.

Kevin knew all this. He handed me the letter.

"An invitation like this comes along once in a lifetime, Hoppy," Kevin said. "Maybe you and Joe should take him up on it, since you're headed in that direction anyhow."

I read the letter to Joe over the phone. "Write the guy," he said. "Tell him we're coming!"

What no one knew was that for me Peru had been nearly ruined by the love I left behind.

(There is no such thing as leaving your love behind. Love clings to you more tightly than your own skin does.)

While rejoicing in the South American adventure, my longing for Lucinda Eliott imprisoned me in an agony of despair which I could not express, not even to my best friend.

I was living in two worlds. Half of me was traveling over the Andes and down the jungle rivers of Peru; the other half I'd left back in New Jersey.

In Lima Joe and I had rented a room on the roof of the Pensión Americana on Carabaya, not far from Plaza San Martín. Black vultures roosted right outside the door. Each evening, after we had spent most of the day at the Ministry of Agriculture learning about coffee, I raced up the stairs to see if there was a letter.

Joe knew I was living in a delirium. He saw me taking the steps three at a time, scattering the vultures. If he was worried my passion for Lucy might derail the European project, he didn't give it away. He must have been stoically waiting for the whole thing to blow over.

After that fateful decision in Yurimaguas I went straight to the post office and sent her a cable. Then Joe and I boarded a steamboat (*vapor*) down the Marañón River to Iquitos, arriving a week later. In Iquitos a goldsmith made for me a pendant from a green jade-like stone with a thread of gold running through it, which I had picked up on the bank of the Huallaga River. The chain he fashioned from a bit of Inca gold I had found on an archeological dig.

Lucy was thrilled I was coming home. She would take some time off from college so we could be together. I ran to the airline office, made a reservation and sent another telegram. She cabled back that she would meet my plane in New York. She was planning to throw a homecoming party for me at her parents' home in New Jersey.

I fell in love with Lucinda Eliott when she was 18 years old. I was 21, nearly 22, and had just graduated from Princeton, or was about to graduate. I had known her, or about her, all my life because we grew up in the same small community in New Jersey. Our parents were friends, and we had both gone to the Peck School. I didn't pay any attention to her at Peck. When you're 13 or 14, a four-year gap is enormous, and she was still a child when I went away to the Hotchkiss School in Connecticut. At Peck she was the most outstanding student in her class.

Over the next few years I saw her across the dance floor at the Christmas Cotillions at the country club, where young people of different age groups mixed. When I was 18 or 19, she was 14 or 15 and already tall for her age. (She would grow to be 5' 9".) You couldn't help noticing her large blue eyes, her long blonde hair, but most of all her stunning figure. She was invariably the center of attention. Somebody called her a "ripe peach, ready for plucking." Boys in their last year of boarding school or first year of college sometimes "took over" the best-looking younger girls at these parties. We flattered them, or thought we did, by dancing with them, inviting them to sit at our tables, and feeding them drinks to get them drunk. By the end of the evening, however, we usually tired of these "discoveries" and went on to another party with girls our own age.

To remember exactly when I fell in love or was first smitten, I have to work backwards from my graduation from Princeton because she attended and spent the night before with me in my room but not, I'm sorry to say, in the same bed. Her parents had allowed her to do this. I don't know why. I thought it was very risqué. She seemed to have a lot of freedom. Her parents must have trusted her. Perhaps, because they were friends of my parents, they trusted me. Had they known what forces of love and lust were raging in my heart they would have insisted on a chastity belt and a chaperone. Perhaps they divined I was in love with their daughter, and in those days love protected a girl.

We must have met at a dance over Easter vacation, because I remember inviting her to a spring weekend at Princeton. She was a senior at Farmington in Connecticut and couldn't get out. Our first date must have been in June, because she was home from school. I drove to her house on Holland Road in Far Hills, New Jersey, where her mother and father greeted me like a long-lost son.

Down the stairs she came, the all-American girl, already suntanned, dressed in a summer frock and sandals with a sweater carelessly thrown over her shoulders. Her finger- and toenails were painted bright pink. The starry eyes, flowing blonde hair and fabulous figure, which I had to keep from staring at, practically took my breath away. With looks and a body like that she belonged on a surfboard, but no, she had graduated top of her class at Farmington, and was on her way to Radcliffe.

Like her parents, she seemed radiantly happy to see me. Their enthusiasm was bewildering.

In those days I was still driving my old robin's-egg-blue Ford convertible. Chatty, friendly and warm, she sat, not on the far end of the front seat by the door, but discreetly near me, close enough to touch but not touching. We were, after all, without ever having spent any time together, old friends. That our families had known each other for years, plus the fact that we had grown up in the same community and gone to the same school, gave us a sense of intimacy. We had lots of things to talk about. The awkward-first-date blues were not for us.

We drove to Lambertville to hear a Louis Armstrong concert. On the way she told me that she had just read a book about phrenology (a new word for me) and claimed that she could tell me things about myself by feeling the shape and contours of my skull.

"Go ahead," I challenged, wondering what was coming next.

What she said about my character completely eludes me. She was on her knees beside me, tenderly pressing and squeezing my head in a way that was sensuous and sexy but which, since it was not sex but science, seemed to me ingenious. It was a way of touching in a manner that was permitted. She could have done it, I suppose, in front of her parents as a kind of parlor game, like charades. We weren't necking or petting or screwing (God forbid!) on our first date. We were touching and laughing and getting to know each other as we drove through the soft, green New Jersey countryside. She wasn't squeezing my knee; she was caressing my scalp, a singularly unsexy part of the anatomy. I thought it was sensational because it was so unexpectedly clever, a way of breaking the rules without doing anything wrong.

I can still see Louis Armstrong, center stage in Lambertville's summer stock tent, blowing toward heaven on his golden horn. However, I didn't pay much attention to him or my favorite music. I was only aware of the ravishing creature by my side and the feeling of wonder and astonishment swelling in my heart.

A few days after graduation, life, in the form of plans that each of us had made before we – I mean I – fell in love, intervened. I had enrolled in the University of Madrid for a summer course in Spanish before going to Peru. Lucy was also bound for Europe, to tour the continent with a choral group from Farmington. We promised to meet in London at the end of the summer. I cannot remember how we said goodbye.

I flew to London, bought a Triumph motorcycle, and rode to Madrid. The next two months are more or less a blank in my mind as I waited out our enforced term of separation.

At the end of the course I sped through Spain and France, past cathedrals and castles, and arrived in London about midnight, where I checked into a bed and breakfast behind Victoria station. In the morning I put on what was left of the suit I had had made in Madrid (the trousers lay in a ditch somewhere between Burgos and San Sebastián) and set out for the Half Moon Hotel off Piccadilly.

I was told that she had gone with her group to Canterbury for the day. After having nearly killed myself a couple of times on my ride across Europe, the prospect of having to wait a few more hours was intolerable. I had looked forward to this rendezvous all summer. Although we had not set a time, I was angry with her for not being there to meet me.

I pulled out some money to pay for *Time* magazine and, in my frustration, ripped my wallet in two. I skulked around the entrance to the hotel like a surly tomcat. When the doorman grew suspicious, I went off to Green Park.

When you are in love and waiting for your lover, everything else, the suffering of others in particular, seems irrelevant. I spent the day moving restlessly among the deckchairs and benches in Green Park, reading with indifference about tragedies occurring in other parts of the world, and anxiously scrutinizing everybody who walked down Piccadilly.

Suddenly, like an apparition that I had conjured through sheer force of concentration, there she was, walking through the trees.

The first thing I noticed was that she was wearing a cape – some continental frivolity – over her shoulders. We saw each other at the same moment, but she took the initiative. While I stood rooted to the ground, she was already running. She threw her arms around me, like they do in the movies.

In spite of this rapturous beginning, we soon discovered that our separate summer experiences had estranged us. An intangible wall divided us at the very moment when we wanted to renew our intimacy.

During dinner her fingertips darted like flames as she recounted her European adventures. While I listened, I tried to fight off the feeling that all was lost. There had been boys in the choral group, something I hadn't suspected. The Farmington choir had joined up with one from Deerfield Academy. Either she had forgotten this detail, or had deliberately neglected to tell me. My perch at the top of the ladder was being challenged. A cold sense of resignation spread through my veins like an anesthetic.

I remember thinking, "It's over. It was just a summer romance. In a month she'll be at Radcliffe, and I'll be in the jungles of Peru. Better to get it over with here and now. Why prolong the agony?"

At the same time I was determined not to let love die, and so, I discovered, was she.

There was no place to hug or kiss, which was what we both desperately wanted to do. I had no car, and we were in a city. So we got on the motorcycle, which saved us because, as every enthusiast of two wheels knows, you can't really talk on a motorcycle, but you can hug. That is, she can hug you, and the faster you drive, the tighter she'll squeeze. And there are ways of hugging back, of letting her know how much you love her caresses.

We spent half the night riding around London. A motorcycle is one of the best ways to get around a city, and the best time to see a city is at night, especially late at night. We had both: the warm August night, and the Bonneville purring between our knees.

So little time remained before we would go our separate ways. We were in London; this was going to be our last night together. It was like a wartime romance. She nestled her head against the back of my neck with her arms around my middle as we threaded through the theater crowds milling around Piccadilly. We watched but didn't talk as we circled Trafalgar Square and headed up the Mall toward Buckingham Palace. Silence saved us from the reality to which our dinner conversation had sent us tumbling – that our romance was nearly over.

The next day she went off with her group to Edinburgh to tour the Highlands and trace her Scottish past. I sold the bike, did some shopping and, resigned to the fact that things between us were finished, flew back to New York.

Lucy arrived a few days later. David Callard, another Ivy clubmate of mine, was getting married, and I invited her to the wedding. She bounced down the stairs in the same frock she had worn on our first date, and suddenly – it was like a miracle because we both knew it instantly – we were back where we had left off in June. Perhaps our love only flourished in a car, in the state of New Jersey. She got in and threw her arms around me. Heart pounding with happiness, I drove to the church.

The ceremony was a blur; I hardly knew or cared what was going on. Once again, I was only conscious of a delirious sensation within me and of the beautiful young woman who clung to my arm. Lucy, in my eyes, was by far the prettiest girl at the wedding.

The heady sexual atmosphere of the wedding party was contagious. When we weren't dancing we were rolling on the lawn at the bottom of the garden, beneath the trees. Lucy was embarrassed by the grass stains on her dress, but I was proud of them, as though I had deflowered her. (I never would.)

I had planned to spend Labor Day weekend with my family before leaving for Peru. At the wedding I asked Lucy to come with me. She asked her parents for permission. They gave it, and we set off for East Hampton.

That week I remember as one of the happiest of my life. Lucy was not the sporty type; that is, she did not participate in competitive games. Nevertheless, she walked with me to the tennis club and followed me around the golf course, book in hand. She had set herself a prodigious summer reading list for Radcliffe – English classics which I had heard of but not read. Everything I did, she wanted to do. If I got up early to bike to the beach for a pre-breakfast swim, she made me promise to take her. I tiptoed into her room and woke her with a warm embrace before we dashed to the beach for a freezing plunge into the ocean.

She even managed to befriend and neutralize my jealous little sister. She did this by inviting Susie to accompany us to every nightclub and party we went to. I was aghast at the prospect of having little sister along to spy on us. Fortunately, Susie had the good sense to refuse. She still felt included because every morning at breakfast Lucy made a point of filling her in on where we'd been and who we'd seen the evening before. When Susie drew me aside and whispered, "Do you really think you should go to Peru?" I knew Lucy had won.

Our sexual intimacy increased from day to day. I had already told her a thousand times that I loved her, and went on repeating it with every breath and sentence. She never told me that she loved me, but I was 90 percent certain that she did. What else could explain those passionate embraces, her eagerness to go with me everywhere, and the fact she hung on my every word? That increment of uncertainty, however, kept me in a constant state of emotional arousal and expectation.

We were living from moment to moment. Our paths were about to diverge. Our destinies lay in foreign lands, not in New Jersey. Lucy was about to embark on a distinguished academic career at Radcliffe. In a matter of days I would be off to seek my fortune in the jungles of Peru. We were both eager to get on with our lives. We discussed the future, but it was not a joint future. We tacitly agreed we would wait and see.

I cannot remember how we said goodbye. When we spoke on the phone for the last time, she told me to find the book she had given me and open it to the last page. After hanging up the phone I ran to the book. She had written the words,

I love you, Johnny. I'm going to guard my love for you in a secret place in my heart until you come back.

It's hard to describe the euphoric effect this inscription had on me. My happiness was almost more that I could contain. It was as though I had been given an injection of a powerful, ecstasy-inducing drug. Every few minutes I ran back to the book to reread the words, to have my joy renewed and elation topped up.

When my flight from Lima reached Miami, the passengers were informed that a blizzard had hit New York. The plane, after a considerable delay, continued as far as Washington.

In Washington it was snowing hard. I taxied to Union Station and caught the last train for New York. It inched northwards and stopped for several hours in Philadelphia; then part of it – two or three cars – headed off into the storm. I was shivering in my tropical suit and beset by a mood of disorientation and despair. Clutching a palm-wood bow and hollow fishing arrows six feet in length which I had bought from an Indian trader in Iquitos, I counted the little flares that had been lit by the switches to keep them from freezing. The homecoming party must have already been in full swing. When would I see her again? She had to go back to Radcliffe the next day. Hope was fading like those flickering flares in the snowy night.

The train got as far as Princeton Junction, where my parents met me. I wanted to go straight to the party, but the hour was late, it was snowing hard, and the roads were bad. We were lucky to get home.

The next morning I called her. She described the party, and how disappointed everyone was that I wasn't there. She sounded preoccupied. It was Sunday, and she was worried about getting back to college. I wanted to drive her, but we were snowed in. I felt like a man who had once held a handful of gold dust, only for it to run through his fingers. Only a few grains remained.

The next weekend I put my skis on the top of the car and drove north. At Radcliffe I was an outsider. This wasn't my college. Having gone to a men-only university, I felt awkward asking women for directions. Besides, my experiences in South America had hardened me. I was eager to get back on the road; Joe and I were already making plans to go to Africa. After the jungles of Peru, academia seemed predictable, almost nauseatingly tame.

Lucy was absorbed by her studies. Her face was pale from long hours in the library. And there were, she admitted, other men in her life. She was dating a senior at Harvard. One of her professors had asked her to dinner. He was introducing her to his colleagues. Naturally she was flattered by this attention, and intrigued by the more intellectual circles in which she was already beginning to move.

We drove to Wilmington, Vermont, and stayed in separate rooms in a country inn. Lucy did not ski. She had brought along several books to read. The weather turned warm. A thaw set in, and it began to rain. The dirty melting snow did nothing to lift our spirits.

By now I was convinced that she no longer loved me – at least not with the same abandon as she had last summer. I felt weak, as though the blood had run out of my veins.

Everything I said had the ring of awkward desperation. I slipped on the ice and twisted my ankle. Without her love, I was no better than a cripple. I staggered around like an amputee attempting to take his first steps on wooden legs. Nothing could compensate for the emptiness I felt.

What was there between us now? I tried to describe the deep happiness she had brought me, but was tongue-tied with despair. I couldn't get the words out.

Rilke: "Lovers, are you still the same?" We were definitely not. Should we have simply been content to say *Erat hora*, and turn away? Were we granted, like Rihaku's paired butterflies, just a few hours in the sun and no more?

I had wanted to know everything about Lucy, to learn her every facet, and for her to know me in every way for better and for worse, inside and out. But I felt so inhibited that I was hardly able to speak. I did not want to be friends with her; I wanted us to be lovers. Whether we would have ever married or not seemed unimportant, but friendship would have been, for me, second best.

There were brief moments of tenderness, of talking and touching through the bars that had grown up between us, but it was the happiness of a condemned man whose love had only hours to live. On Sunday we returned to Cambridge and said goodbye.

I drove back to New Jersey in a state of confused despair. Love, with Time stirring, Love, which had seemed such a deep, potent elixir, had dissolved to nothingness. Yet among the dying embers one bright flame flickered: I had been released to embark on an unparalleled African adventure.

But the half-life of love is forever.

The pendant stayed in my pocket.

*   *   *

On March 29, Joe and I boarded the *Saturnia* for the 14-day trip (and 14 sleepless nights) to Naples. I don't remember sleeping a wink the whole way. Either the slow-changing time zones screwed up my body clock, or was it the sound of water sluicing by the bulkhead? We were in a third-class cabin, below the waterline, shared with several others.

I became a member of a group of somnambulists who wandered – zombie-like – the decks and staterooms of the *Saturnia* from midnight until dawn. Many were children, who had apparently crept from the family cabin while their parents slept. Nobody spoke, we became nodding acquaintances as we came to recognize each other from our sleep wanderings night after night. My peregrinations inevitably led upwards from steerage to first class, where the only man on duty was the bartender, happy to have a customer at 4 a.m.

The *Saturnia* finally docked in Naples, home of pizza and the laundry line. Never in my life had I seen so much wash hanging out. The alley cats squalled all night, fighting or fornicating on the rooftops around our *pensione*.

We trained south to Paestum to visit the temples. This part of Italy was once part of Magna Graecia, one of the colonies established by Greek city states around 800 BC. Paestum was eventually abandoned because of malaria and incessant internecine quarrels. We got off the train in the middle of nowhere, just a little shack with the word PAESTUM on a sign. The day was hot and the land flat, with waist-high fields of artichokes in every direction. I had never seen artichokes growing before. These were baby ones, about halfway between a baseball and a golf ball, the size Italians relish.

We could see the temples in the distance above the artichokes, swimming in the super-heated air. They were not ivory white, but made of a kind of grayish-brown stone, all in perfect condition. We had the place to ourselves.

Those were magic moments, sprawled on the warm stones of the fully intact temples dedicated to Demeter and Poseidon. Butterflies fluttered about, and a myriad of insects pollinating the flowers. The inventors of democracy seemed to have only recently departed. In the distance the sea shimmered and beckoned. No one came to disturb the peace and tranquility we shared with 3,000 years of history.

We trained to Rome, and settled at the Pensione Forte, on via Margutta, near the Spanish Steps. We ate our meals at Taverna Margutta, where I discovered calves' brains fried in butter. I was still tortured by the insomnia acquired aboard the *Saturnia*; as a consequence I managed to finish *Swann's Way*.

Proust was Joe's bible. He'd read the whole thing while he was in the army.

At Princeton he was known as "Rebel," not just because he came from the Deep South: he kept a motorcycle hidden in a garage off campus, which he rode into New York to see Tennessee Williams' plays. A star in the English department, his intellectual reputation made him a big man on campus, which was unheard of for someone who was not a top athlete.

In Peru he had said, "Johnny, you have just graduated from one of the finest universities in America, and you are illiterate."

It was true. At Princeton I had concentrated on my political-science courses and had barely cracked a novel. He set me a rigorous reading course beginning with Thomas Mann's *The Magic Mountain*. I think Joe compared me to Mann's hero, Hans Castorp, who goes up the mountain knowing very little, and comes back down a great deal wiser. This was followed by such classics as *The Brothers Karamazov*, *Anna Karenina*, and, his personal favorite, *Lord Jim*. I had been pushed in at the deep end and, to my astonishment, gobbled them up and begged for more. It was a pleasure I had been denying myself for years. We discussed these books on our endless tramps through the slums of Lima, late at night in the dives around the Plaza de Armas, and sprawled on the beach, dazed and refreshed from plunging beneath mammoth Pacific rollers. Along with the excitement and adventure of seeking our fortunes in the jungle, Peru for me was truly a monumental learning experience. All thanks to Joe.

At the American Express office near the Spanish Steps I received a letter from Sam with all kinds of tips on how to get to Kenya. Plane direct to Nairobi. By freighter via Suez. Around Cape Horn. But we had already made up our minds how we were going to travel: by motorcycle. We checked out the Italian models: Ducati. They looked fast but somehow untrustworthy. First we wanted to see more of Italy.

Every day we scanned the English-language newspapers for jobs to keep us going. In the *Rome Daily American* I spotted an ad that looked promising:

WANTED:

READER FOR A BLIND ENGLISH WRITER.

ROOM AND BOARD. TEL. 47146

I made the call. An English voice answered. Name: Jocelyn Lubbock. His elderly uncle needed a companion and reader. I said there was not just one, but two of us. Both Princeton graduates. All the better, he said.

We trained to La Spezia. We were met at the station by Jocelyn, a gray-haired gentleman about 40, nephew of Percy Lubbock, a distinguished man of letters. (Joe had never heard of him.) We could tell he was fairly desperate to find a reader for the old man, who was very demanding and had sent a series of mainly women readers packing back to England almost the day each of them arrived.

We had no idea what to expect. Shack or chateau?

The latter. Villa Medici was tucked away in an olive grove and perched on a promontory (Gli Scafari) overlooking the Golfo de La Spezia. Elena opened the door to high ceilings and marble floors. Jocelyn led the way upstairs to meet the great man. He was sunk in a wheelchair on the loggia, overlooking the sea, which he could hear and smell but no longer see. Our arrival perked him up. Mario pulled him up straight in the chair. Percy was drawn to Joe's southern accent, and asked if he would read Tennessee Williams' plays. Joe said he would do so with pleasure, and described his motorcycle rides to New York.

Preceded by cocktails, lunch was served al fresco. First course: baby artichokes! Followed by seafood pasta and strawberries. Strong coffee. Plenty of Italian wine. Mario was our bartender. He was also a fisherman. He caught those fish.

Percy: "Every Italian strawberry wishes it were a Kent strawberry."

After lunch came the hour of the siesta. Mario wheeled Percy away, and Jocelyn showed us our room: two huge four-posters draped with mosquito netting, marble floors, views over the Golfo. We thought we'd hit paradise.

Our daily routine:

At 11 o'clock Mario wheeled Percy onto the loggia. For an hour or so I read from the pink, lightweight airmail edition of the London *Times*, which miraculously arrived early each morning. After that I used my newly acquired Italian to read from one of the Italian newspapers. We chatted about America and England and the literary figures he knew and admired or did not admire. He knew E.M. Forster when they both worked at a military hospital in Cairo in 1915, and Rupert Brooke. He was a friend of Henry James and Edith Wharton. Percy was a mine of literary gossip going back 50 years. James' pocket watch and chain were produced for our inspection.

From perusing his shelves I gathered that his titles included *The Craft of Fiction* and *Shades of Eton*.

I came across an article in the paper that said that Aldous Huxley's house in California had burned to the ground, with his archives and papers in it.

Percy positively rejoiced.

"Serves him right for writing such rubbish."

Brave New World.

Reading was followed by pre-lunch drinks – Campari soda, gin and tonic, etc. Joe appeared from a swim in the sea, and Percy declared that he could smell the brine on his body. He clearly enjoyed the company of young men. Then another delicious pasta lunch from Elena's kitchen, wheeled out by Mario on a trolley. Lunch was followed by the inevitable siesta, during which Joe and I headed down to the rocks. We had bought snorkels and flippers, and explored the waters around Gli Scafari.

At four in the afternoon Joe took over (T. Williams). This was the longest session. At seven cocktails were served, followed by dinner, maybe followed by a "settling" Scotch or brandy. After dinner another session. It was my turn again now. By ten o'clock the old boy was ready for bed. Mario answered the bell and wheeled our host away, prepared him for the night. Percy had a huge paunch, but his legs were weak from lack of use. Mario was strong, smiling and strong: he and Elena had a good deal there.

The next day our hours were reversed. Joe started off; then I took over, etc.

SUNDAY, JUNE 11, 1961, LERICI, ITALY, 3 P.M.

On this day in June, the day of my sister Susie's debutante party in N.J., one week after Percy's 82nd birthday, I find myself sitting in my bathing suit on a rock off a headland known as Gli Scafari in the Mediterranean. I have come here for 24 hours – one day and one night – and have brought the following items:

SLEEPING BAG	UNDERWEAR
AIR MATTRESS	20 CIGARETTES
BATHING SUIT	2 PACKS MATCHES
RUBBER PARKA	2 BALLPOINT PENS
SOCKS	THIS NOTEBOOK

TOWEL SWISS ARMY KNIFE

SWEATER MEDIHALER SPRAY

BLUE JEANS WRISTWATCH

TURTLENECK SHIRT FLASHLIGHT

T-SHIRT

CANVAS SHOES

LEATHER STRAP

I hand-paddled the air-filled rubber mattress (the English call it a "lilo") with the above items packed in a plastic bag under my chin. It is three o'clock in the afternoon. I have been here 45 minutes.

This was Percy's idea. During one of our reading sessions, I mentioned that I had kept a diary of our adventures in Peru, how much I enjoyed doing that, and was beginning to think about becoming a writer. He said that to test my resolve I should come out to this rocky islet, stay completely alone for 24 hours, and think, meditate, fast (I have brought neither food nor water), and write down whatever comes into my head.

The only thing between me and this broad, flat yellow rock is the "lilo," my bed for the night. Very pleasant to be nearly naked and warm in the sun. Peace pervades me as I listen to the sound of the sea bumping and nudging the rocks beneath.

Joe will be reading in my place this evening. Now he is watching me from the rocks below Villa Medici. He is not waving or shouting, just gazing and wondering.

Joe desperately searches his heart and soul for meaning. He is troubled while I, on the other hand, must seem to him, in spite of my chaotic family history... fairly serene. Like a mole, he tunnels toward confrontation. He thrives on it; it is the one thing I do my best to avoid. It satisfies him, but it wearies me. Me, I've had enough of confrontation. Only two years separate us, but he is my teacher, and I am his first student. I am content to stay on the sidelines with my pen and notebook. He watches while I write it all down. If I don't, the amazing experiences we have already shared in less than one year may get lost. Besides, writing brings peace. Sanity. Solitude and distance are what I need. They contribute a semblance of order to the whirlwind life we have been leading. Six months ago I was drifting down the upper Amazon on a balsa raft; now we are going to paddle up the Nile!

Hot now.

4 P.M.

I have been swimming, and the body feels comfortable in the sun. With my knife I prized a handful of mussels (*cozze* in It.) from the rock. I wedged them open, one by one, slicing through the hinge, scraped out the still live animals and swallowed them whole.

The rocks here are jagged and sharp: I scratched my knee as I hauled myself out of the water. With this heavy yet predictable swell, you have to wait until it sweeps you up to a place that you can cling to, then clamber up on one of the ledges while the water recedes.

The taste of these mussels is not much different from the raw clams they serve at the Oyster Bar in Grand Central Station in New York, which is where this adventure got started.

Soon it will be the cocktail hour at the villa, our favorite hour to be with Percy, with dinner served on the loggia. But I am content here. Peaceful with the vibrant murmuring and thumping of the sea as it claws and sucks at the rocks.

Smoked one cigarette. Good taste after the salty swim.

5 P.M.

We have been looking for what Percy calls the "Eton fish," a black and blue denizen that comes out only at night. So far no sightings, even though we swim with lights.

6 P.M.

My coming to spend a few hours in complete solitude on this rock was also inspired by a book I have just read: *Siddhartha* by Hermann Hesse. It's a young man's book. This book is remarkable in many ways, and will require more than one reading. I was struck by the extraordinary control the Samanas exert over their bodies. The soul gains control over body and senses. Indeed, the Samanas abhor the sensual world. Such mind-over-body control is unknown in the Western world.

The lesson Siddhartha learned is that wisdom cannot be obtained from another: it must spring from personal experience. Like from this rock.

But Joe and I have a lot to learn from each other. We have already — mostly I from him. We complement each other. A good traveling companion is hard to find. Without him I would never have attempted this epic voyage that awaits us.

6:30 P.M.

The sun is going down, faster now. No hunger or thirst. Not yet. Just boredom.

Bugs are crawling all over this rock, perhaps attracted by the shattered mussel shells, which I now scrape into the sea. The ones with wings are biting — sent to try our patience, as Percy would say.

The Germans in their camping ground are having supper. That's where the lovely Sonia dwells, with her mother, in a tent.

> We watched the ocean and sky together,
> Under the roof of blue Italian weather.
>
> SHELLEY

Ah, the sun has momentarily reappeared from beneath a cloud before bidding goodnight. The bay, even the German camp, and especially Tellaro are all beautiful now.

I was glad to read Joe's poetry last night, even though I couldn't fathom it. Delicacy infringed upon by chaos. When did delicacy ever win against chaos? Only when reinforced by determination. In Joe, delicacy and chaos may have become allies, maybe.

I hope Susie's party will be a grand success. I hope my unhappy sister will find a man to take her away. The divorce changed our lives forever and she, being the youngest, the only one still at home, suffered the most when the earth shook, and all that she had thought secure started crumbling beneath her.

7 P.M.

The last bathers are leaving the rocks across the cove. I alone am left. Not much of a sunset – choked off by clouds. These bugs are eating me alive. Some raindrops on my arm – could be a bad night ahead.

I am reminded by this rain, the biting bugs, and this orange parka of my first night on the Huallaga River in Peru. Miserable night that (in December), alone on a parked balsa while Juan and Ossorio visited an Indian village in the jungle. I stayed behind with my .38 revolver to guard the cargo (beer). That river trip seems very clear to me now. Seven days on the Huallaga from Tingo María to Bellavista.

Now we are on the Italian shore, lapped by this magical sea of a hundred blue hues. My quarters have been upgraded from muddy Amazonian riverbank to Italian villa. And we are planning a trip across Africa! God, we are moving fast! Not too fast, and not too haphazardly, I hope. The voyage ahead already seems engraved in stone. A monumental fate we cannot avoid.

One thing about the divorce: my mother and father still love us passionately and are riddled with guilt over the misery they have caused.

"So you and Joe want to go to South America and buy a coffee plantation in the Peruvian jungle (while all your friends are getting jobs in banks or business or going to law school and getting married)? What a great idea!"

"And now you want to cross Africa by motorcycle. Sure! That's fine!"

They feel too guilty to say no. They're afraid I'd run away. Now they're worried I won't come back.

More drizzle. Must shield this notebook with the sleeve of my shirt.

8 P.M.

Feeling alone and isolated here. Almost as much as on the Huallaga, which I now look back on as a turning point in my life. That river made me an explorer; this rock will make a writer of me, maybe. Joe and Percy are on the loggia. Joe has turned up the Victrola and is shouting that Elena has prepared calamari and *spaghetti alle vongole* – all from Mario's boat and my favorites. Joe is taunting me to come back and shouts that Percy says no mosquito ever wrote a novel.

8:45 P.M.

Dark now (writing by flashlight). The lighthouse has begun its flickering rounds. Three flashes in five seconds, then dark for eight seconds. Approx. four revolutions per minute. As the sea quiets, the regular thumps subside: what remains is the monotonous washing.

The fishing boats are heading out for the night. Putt-putt-putt they go as their lights search the depths. Four cigarettes gone. Many clouds. Looks like rain. I have all my clothes on and feel ready to face the night. Ugh! What I took to be flakes of scab on my finger, where I cut it yesterday, when examined under flashlight turn out to be a colony of tiny bugs chewing on the wound and gulping my blood.

Cold and damp now.

Now the lights have come on. At Porto Venere across the bay, at Tellaro, in the house, and in the German camp where Sonia will be bedding down beside her protective mother.

The bug brigade have sent in their heavy bombers. The shaft of my flashlight catches them like German aircraft in searchlights during the Battle of Britain. Peaceful now. I am not tired and do not expect much sleep tonight.

Goodnight, sun. You are gone. You are shining in other lands and on other people. I hope you will shine on my sister.

I follow the headlights of cars. Difficult to see now, except by flashlight, which attracts more bugs. I know what the people I left behind are doing. Will they ever find out what I am doing? Maybe through this notebook. Maybe.

Good night. *Bonne nuit. Buenas noches. Buona notte.*

My eyes must be deceiving me. My Peruvian poncho seems to be giving off some green light.

Good night!

MONDAY, JUNE 12

Wide awake and up at 4:15 a.m. – already bright but approaching dark clouds portend rain. Someone just went off to work on his motorcycle. Must be the milkman.

Slept quite well – as well as I could in a sleeping bag. Both shoulders sore. Fishing boats putt-putting out for a day's work.

No hunger or thirst yet. Just a hollow feeling in the stomach.

8:45 A.M.

Slept again from five until eight. Early morning snoozes are the best. Woke up stiff in all my joints, plus a headache.

Went for a swim and did some loosening-up exercises. Better now.

Morning heavily clouded – drab and dreary and made worse by the sound of bulldozers working on the road. Joe has been watching through field glasses.

10 A.M.

I have learned something new about this rugged pile of rocks. There is an underwater tunnel beneath it, right under where I am sitting now. Down there the water pulses back and forth with each successive wave. But when the waves meet in the middle, the shudder from the impact can be felt all through the rock.

It's odd to see Joe or Elena waving from the house. They seem to have drifted away. Or maybe it's me who's done the drifting. He who returns from a solitary venture is not the same man who left. You can't stick your foot into the same river twice, and so forth.

Have these hours on the rock taught me anything? I do want to go on experimenting with fasting and solitude. Africa. The hours have passed quickly. A few twinges of boredom. Nothing like solitude and empty time to fill the pages.

I wonder how Susie's party went last night. The family wanted big brother to be there, to escort her. I feel guilty I did not.

11 A.M.

Time to leave. Sea rougher. It looks like a challenge to get off this rock and keep these pages dry.

*   *   *

JUNE 14

So it was a question of *which* motorcycle. In May we took a few days off from our duties and trained from Spezia to Munich. Riding through the fog- and pollution-choked early-morning city in a taxi, we passed a BMW showroom, where Joe spotted a *white* BMW motorcycle glowing like a pearl in the mist. "*That's* the one we want!" he shouted. The taxi screeched to a stop. We had never seen a white BMW before: all the others are black. We went in and for $850 I bought with traveler's checks the beautiful R50 (500 cc) machine plus windscreen, spare tire, and baggage rack.

We said, "We are going to ride this machine across Africa. Can we get some sort of sponsorship?"

Salesman: "Boys, there is nowhere in the world this machine hasn't been; maybe not to the top of Mount Everest."

We rode the machine over the Alps to Italy. Brenner Pass. The feeling was incredible: swooning around Alpine corners, with engine sound as smooth as silk, you soon develop a supreme confidence: brilliantly cambered hairpin turns at 40 mph, 80 on the straights. The cool Alpine air is deflected by the windscreen, but gulped down with ecstasy. Postcard valleys below, glaciers above. Alto Adige. Then down to Italy and vines and olive oil. Goodbye starchy dirndls and hello warm brown bosoms!

In Bologna a local artist painted in black letters the words "The White Nile" on both sides of our snow-white gas tank, because that is the route we have decided to follow across Africa.

*   *   *

S. Small
Impala Farm
P.O. Box 92
Nanyuki
Kenya Colony
B.E.A.
June 10, 1961

John L. Hopkins Jr., Esq.
c/o American Express
Rome, Italy

Presso Lubbock
Gli Scafari
Lerici
REGISTERED

Dear John Hopkins,

Very nice to get your letter from Naples, and to hear that the one I sent to the Club actually made contact as there is an ungodly lot of pilfering or purposeful carelessness in the post these days.

Yes – my offer still holds good, and I'll be delighted to have you both to stay as long as you like – make the place your headquarters and come and go as you please. We're pretty much out in the "blue" – my next civilized neighbor north is Haile Selassie – to the east the Indian Ocean – not so bad in the other directions with Nairobi four hours to the South and the White Highlands to the South and East.

I've nine spare beds, my own poultry, milk, vegetables, etc., and plenty of wogs so it's no pain to put people up if they can stand the low veldt and lack of neighbors. Actually I'd very much welcome some company at the moment as all the adjoining farms are deserted except for livestock. The local police post has been pulled back into the Nanyuki Cantonment, and the cattle raiding has hotted up considerably and I'm having a more or less steady stream of beasts being whipped.

I suppose you realize you are coming into what might be referred to as a *disturbed* area (Kenya) and liable at any moment to get one hell of a lot more disturbed! We are frozen in a legislative crisis at the moment, and no one knows which way the cat will jump. (Has now been resolved – the bloody Governor giving in to the wogs.)

It should be damn interesting for someone who has written *two* theses on Africa – especially one on the Mau Mau. However, *don't* go doing any private investigating till you get *here*, as Americans are not ace high with either the Africans or the British at the moment – especially since "Soapy" Williams' B.S. tour, and the near advent of Kennedy's *Freedom Fighters* or whatever they are called. That means sticking to European or Government transport and *no hitch-hiking*. The Immigration Department has been given carte blanche to turf anyone out at an hour's notice and no reason given, and *they're doing it, what's more*. The Gov. is petrified of having any sort of "International incident" and too many young reporter types plunge into the nearest native quarters and try to get the truth or some such effort and are lucky to escape with their throats unhinged.

I should think the Nile trip would be *far and away* more interesting than the scalding trip through the Red Sea and Canal and Indian Ocean. You'd need an Egyptian Visa, one for both *North* and *South* Sudan, perhaps one will cover both now, and one for British East Africa (on the latter, things are changing so fast that you better make a *damn* good check and see that you don't need separate ones for *Uganda* and *Tanganyika!*). As well as Kenya.

There are steamers beating up and down the Nile with intervals of railroads. The steamers will bring you right to Lake Victoria, and I could pick you up there. They have tiny cabins, fair food, plenty of grog, and really right out of Kipling and you'll see the great Egyptian Temples before the new dam covers them.

Make sure you have all the "shots" (inoculations) going. *Cholera* too as God knows what will erupt out of the Congo and Angola with the breakdown of all medical authority as well as everything else. And with half this country weakened by famine — we'll be easy pickings for *any* germ. If you keep me posted, I might be able to get you brought down from KITALE by some of the Army Garrison Transport. I have some of the Coldstream Guards quartered on me more or less constantly, and I can dig a fair bit of "squeeze" out of them in the way of transport, etc.

There is damn good coffee farming here, but all available land is under European cultivation (except in the native reserves) and expensive as hell. You can certainly buy coffee shambas, but the price has dropped very imperceptibly.

In my turn — I'll be most interested to talk about ranching in South America, as we're all keeping an eye peeled as to where to go if we have to. There is one movement afoot in this district to try to move lock, stock, and barrel via ox-wagon to Abyssinia. (Petrol would be the first thing to give out, and motor transport useless) – driving our cattle and sheep and trying to fight off the Turkana, Somali, Jaingilli raiders with horse commandos. At least we would get to have a possibility of getting out *some* of our assets (the livestock), all of which would have to be left if we go by boat or plane.

Other people are off to Australia and New Zealand, Borneo and New Guinea, S.A., and the ranch lands of Andalusia in Spain and northern Canada.

Sorry this is such a sermon, but am chained down in bed in the hospital with blood-poisoning in one leg, and only just this minute after 2½ weeks have they let me sit up – the other pages were written more or less suspended in mid-air and should be an archaeological feat to decipher as the line of thought was more or less channeled through a lovely fog of morphine.

I am most serious about not getting off the main route of boat or rail or *European* taxi or bus service. There is an unofficial but very heavy tent of censorship over the news of unrest and lawlessness here so you can't possibly have heard a fifth of what is rocking the land, but you should be alright in the above-mentioned modes of travel, and in the European hotels.

If you do run into trouble nip smartly into the nearest Garrison Cantonment – Coldstream *G's* preferably as I know all the officers, or any of the British Regiments – next into a Police Post, or last into a Kings African Rifles post or unit (*last* as they are black troops – white officers). A hotel, bank, or *big* plantation or ranch also make good forting up.

I sound like someone's maiden aunt but things are very dicey. However, there are still loads of tourists, race meetings, rugby matches and dances and polo – Sundowner bands "Beating Retreat" on the Garrison parade grounds. The theater is booming in Nairobi and the good old British "showing the flag" in all directions, and we may – just may pull through.

It's certainly fine to hear that some young Americans have the "get up and git" and do a bit of helling around the world before settling down. I thought it had been submerged by the "gray flannel suit."

Let me know your plans, and what you would like to do and see here, and I can do some tentative reconnoitering. I'm going over to Arabia at some time as I have some Army friends in Aden, Bahrain, and one chap with the Trucial Oman Scouts. If you'd be interested in a quiet trip over and back by R.A.F., let me know and we might wangle something. Visas, I think, we'd forget.

Well, looking forward to both hearing from you and seeing you soon. The rains are over in June (if they ever come to any seriousness) and the weather is more glorious then everywhere. I've a Land Rover, and can get to most places without too much trouble. A Vine character Fig (Francis Coleman) is in our embassy – a friend of mine and a great friend of my brother George; say hello to him from me.

Yours sincerely,

Sam Small

*   *   *

The basic difference between Joe and me was that he was a poet: meaning he sought perfection, while I was a pragmatic opportunist with no ideals. To give an example: our daily routine in Villa Medici – reading to Percy, handling his mail, etc. – sent Joe into fits of despair because he was anxious to get on the road; while I was more than happy to pause in that beautiful villa, reflect a little, study Italian, and do some intensive reading beneath the net. Not forgetting the blessings of sun and sea.

Also: while Joe read I snuck down to the rocks to play with Sonia in the waves. So far she had only let me see her body underwater.

JUNE 15, VILLA MEDICI, LERICI

We have been here nearly two months. Percy receives a steady stream of visitors, all English, who have come to sit at the feet of the great man of letters, to listen to his tales of encounters and friendships with such literary heavyweights as E.M. Forster, Henry James, Edith Wharton, and Bernard Berenson. Lerici has an exotic English literary history – Keats and the Shelleys. Shelley drowned here. Byron is reputed to have swum across the bay, which Percy said was rubbish even though there was a plaque on the other side indicating where the crippled poet presumably hauled himself from the water.

Jocelyn visited to check on the old boy. He reported that Percy said we were the best readers he'd ever had. He was happier than in many blind years and would be sad when we leave (in ten days).

Percy is blind but not color-blind.

Lizzie Watts, a friend from New Jersey who was studying art in Rome, trained up for a visit.

Percy: "That is a pretty red frock you are wearing."

And so it was.

JUNE 16

For Joe Africa holds out the possibility that he might again feel the poetic identity he experienced in Peru. Therein, he feels, lies his only chance of genuine creativity, be it poetry or whatever. Now most of his creative energy is bound up in his seemingly unshakeable devotion to yours truly. All this reliance on our friendship, which he clings to like a drowning man: I'm not sure I can deliver on all his expectations.

She is a strong swimmer, my Sonia. Finally the mermaid consented to come ashore. We had a secret rendezvous in the olive grove after dinner while Joe read to Percy. I had concealed a rolled-up sleeping bag under an olive tree.

JUNE 17

Joe said nothing gave meaning to his life at the moment, except our friendship. Statements like that trouble me. He seems to view us like two lonesome cowboys, riding along forever toward an endlessly receding horizon.

JUNE 19

Sonia didn't turn up for our tryst in the olive grove. I drove the machine to the German camping ground. Their tent was missing. They'd upped sticks and headed back to Lake Constance. Mother didn't want daughter messing around with motorcycle man.

But I am happy to study Italian. Trouble is, it makes me forget my Spanish.

It is rewarding to study a foreign language in a foreign land, esp. the language of that land. You learn a few new words, step out the door, and start using them. Joe is a brilliant teacher, and I am his first student. Creative day, Joe more relaxed, because Sonia has vamoosed.

JUNE 20

Percy's library is shelved in the "sun room," a westward-facing upstairs salon where we do our reading. It is not a huge collection, but eclectically English, with few European or American-authored volumes represented.

I read the books he chooses; we rarely discuss. It is a way of filling the empty hours until we can fill our glasses. Now reading Lionel Trilling's biography of Matthew Arnold. Heavy weather.

Joe is having a livelier time with T. Williams' plays. Percy loves the southern accent. He has never been to America. Joe is the first southerner he has ever met. The Alabama accent lends authenticity to the play. Joe spends half the time describing the Latin Quarter in New Orleans, what life is like down south. It turns out that Percy has a lively interest in the American Civil War. He is fascinated to learn that

one of Admiral ("Full speed ahead! Damn the torpedoes!")
Farragut's cannonballs has been lodged in an ancient live
oak tree near Joe's family home on Mobile Bay since 1864.

JUNE 21

A heavy-duty session with Joe last night. His obsession with
"purity" implies strong undercurrents of shame or guilt.
Frankly, I don't feel either. For me "purity" is not an issue. I
don't use the word "purity" all the time. Unlike Joe, I don't
have any ideals. I've already been through the mill (divorce),
soaked up enough punishment, and am prepared to take
life as it comes, as long as it is distant from my strife-torn
family. Divorce, like shipwreck, makes a survivor of you.
Or not.

Joe thrives on confrontation, while I avoid it. I've had
enough confrontation. Every time I go home I get confrontation. People with hair-trigger tempers wandering around in
an emotional vacuum. Abroad I stand on my own two feet;
at home I am a coward. What I should have said, etc.

I have opted for "the path of least resistance," as my
father would have called it: in other words, "to get the hell
out of Dodge" (leave home and everything that has to do
with home), which has led to this gold mine of personal
experience, thanks largely to Joe. This adventure would
never have gotten off the ground without this intellectual
and emotional powerhouse pushing. He is leading me to art,
maybe to literature. Maybe.

From my point of view, the life we are leading, plus the
expectation of what is to come, seems pretty darn good.
What is this yearning for perfection? To me it seems a rocky
path that can only end in self-flagellation. He is my best

friend and teacher: that's where it ends. Trouble is, Joe's devotion is a powerful force. He puts me up on a pedestal, which is a place where I do not want to be. I am the beneficiary of his devotion, but to be the loved one is, in some ways, a heavy and tiresome burden.

JUNE 24

My tragedy – my parents are divorced. This is not as trite as it may sound. Divorce has become so common, people have become so used to it they fail to detect the damage done below the waterline.

We were a fairly happy family, salvaged from the wreckage of my mother's first marriage. My half-sister Niki and half-brother Jay called my father "Daddy," because he raised the four of us – two stepchildren, my sister Susie, and me. He taught Jay to fish, which probably saved Jay's life. Dad was a devoted family man but not a successful bread-winner. Divorce ruined his life. My mother chucked him out into the cold, away from the family Christmases and birthdays, the arguing, the reconciliations and the love, the family holidays and outings for popsicles. There were plenty of gay divorcées and merry widows about, but he never remarried. My grandmother said he was still in love with my mother. How she earned this fidelity, I'll never know. They stayed on friendly terms because of us children. What went on beneath the surface no one will ever know.

He was replaced by my stepfather, Gurdon W. Wattles, a fabulously successful and generous Wall St. tycoon. When I graduated from Princeton, he gave me $5,000, which allowed me to go away and stay away. This is what Joe and I are living on.

Before we boarded the *Saturnia*, we went to the bank, where I turned the check into traveler's checks. I pushed a pile for him to sign: half for you and half for me. He had not received a dime from his family in Alabama. Peru was cheap, and we hoped Africa would be the same. I paid for the *White Nile* but everything else we split down the middle.

JUNE 25

I am becoming bored with reading. I am ready for action, ready to move, pining for Africa. Joe is on the rock.

This was it – the tip of my beak has finally broken through the eggshell.

Africa – the eager anticipation of travel across wilderness both arid and tropical; the excitement of ideas mingling with exotic adventure – a super-colossal flight of the imagination with the transformation to reality just around the corner.

JUNE 26, VILLA MEDICI

Our farewell dinner with Percy. We have all become very fond of each other. He understands our itch to get back on the road. He cried when we hugged. At dawn we were gone.

*　　*　　*

John L. Hopkins Esq.   Should be off
c/o Lubbock   June 21st!
Gli Scafari
Lerici
Italia

Dear John,

A quick note outside the fumes of the hospital. You sound as if you have the most terrific trip lined up and do I envy you! I'm only afraid that I can't think of anyone I know who hasn't been turfed out of the regions you are traveling through – even the tarts!

I do think you *must* find out *where* and *when* the *wet* seasons are from local authorities. *When* it rains in the desert, there is no desert, only a lake. All I could give you would be "hearsay," and like everything in Africa that is most controversial.

I will scrounge around among the old Sudanese "hands" and see what they have to say. I do know very *positively* that the South Sudanese were the most loyal to the British, but *most chopped* a few years ago, by the north who massacred them most thoroughly. I was in the north of Uganda at the time and saw the remnants trickle down. *But*, once in the south, if you say you are coming down to visit a British Officer and aren't stoned to death at once, you're liable to find an old, venerable Sergeant Major, etc., who will come forth and welcome you with pathetic enthusiasm (I was a Gunner Major, if that's any help) and you must give him a cup of tea, etc., with *you*, which will uphold his self-respect.

I have no right to ask it, but any "old soldiers" that you meet, if you could be most polite to them – just respectful as equals, etc. I think you would do a sad world a hell of a lot of good. There are so many who wait for the return of the British Raj, and by gosh are they *gents*.

The "*Effendi*" type you must sort out for yourselves, but the old gent in a blanket and not much else who shuffles in and salutes you, is not just a hanger on but maybe one of the lads who stood firm next to a young Churchill in the long ago *Omdurman* campaign.

I'm afraid I'm most prejudiced on the "South" Sudanese, and some day I'll tell you why.

When you hit us, again I can be of no help *but*, I've given your name to the Coldstream Guards who are "around and about" and any and all of them know me. The next *Regiment* are the *S.A.S. – Special Airborne Service* whom I know from Colonel "John Slim" to the privates. John's father is Field Marshal Said Slim and they are "ready, willing, and able." You could always find a welcome there.

The Royal Horse Artillery – I have a few friends there, but not many. I'd lean on the Coldstream and perhaps the King's African Rifles but I wouldn't choose the latter.

SOME RANDOM SUGGESTIONS

I. As you probably know, the Sudan is having a *terrific and major epidemic* of polio – so I'd certainly get whatever inoculation is going completed at once.

II. There is also a major epidemic of spinal meningitis – 500 dying a week, for what that is worth. (This is the Sudan.)

III. Carry some very potent "anti-diarrhea" medicine as

everyone gets "African tummy" – also something for *dysentery*.

IV. Religiously take *anti-malaria* prophylaxis. (Can't spell for beans.)

V. Don't swim in the Nile as it's full of *bilharzia* (a liver fluke) – also crocs who swipe you into the water with their tail if you stand on the edge of the bank as well as thump you in the water.

VI. Have *cholera* shots (inoculations) as I wouldn't be at all surprised to see it break out with all these other epidemics.

VII. As of yesterday – June 17 – Uganda and Kenya have closed the Karamojong – top province – north in British East Africa (over 6,000 head of cattle stolen, and a couple of hundred people killed in the last few months) – so you'll have to do that bit by riverboat which is really very nice.

VIII. I've asked the Royal Automobile Club for a reverse route from here and will forward you the data (as far as Egypt) for what that is worth. At least you can correlate the issue a bit.

IX. If you have any heavy luggage you want to send out, I can put it through the Customs in Nairobi and bring it up and store it here. I have a guest cottage with a couple of bedrooms, bath, and a separate living room of sorts to which I'll give you the key, and you can come and go as you please, and store anything there for as long as you're out here. Have your food with me as I have a good garden and all sorts of game, birds, and of course beef, etc. Just use it as a hotel. Actually whenever you want some spare cash it should be fairly easy to get a temporary job.

x. "Bird dogging" on various people's ranches. The pay wouldn't be enormous, but it would be "all found," and you wouldn't have to know anything about farming. Lots of people often want an extra man on the place for a month or so.

The roads from here to South Africa are very good (for Africa) so you could always hell off there when you've nothing better to do – see the Rhodesias, etc.

This has been written on my knee all over the lot, and the English is vile. The writing worse (*most* seems to have been my favorite word). We've had a gay week – raided last Monday and four steers whipped. I'm still tied to the gharry but manage to get all over the farm. The bastards were too sharp for us and slipped over the border. Then on Wednesday a couple of lads took off from Nanyuki in a light plane, and the whole countryside started a search and it went on till Saturday. I started carrying medicines and bandages and ended up with a shovel, but at noon on Sat. they strolled into Nanyuki having pranged on Mount Kenya, and walked out – a pretty good effort. I was quartering this place in the Land Rover with an R.A.F. plane over me, and he started to "dive bomb" me, wig-wag, etc., and I first decided that he was mad or drunk, and then I realized he was doing everything a twin-engine job could do to sheepdog me home where I get the news that my fattest stock had been attacked by raiders, so off I went, and am sitting in the bush writing this on the bonnet of the gharry.

No real local news – a great "oath taking" about 50 miles away from me in the forest. You undoubtedly read of the shocking murder of Mrs. Osborne. Zanzibar was a great do, and still simmering as is the whole Coast Province. Went to the Queen's Birthday Parade at Government House in Nairobi which was most impressive as well as sad – tears streaming down people's faces men and women alike – as it is probably the last. Armyworms have eaten all the maize and grass, and we are in for a real disaster – last year's famine will be child's play. I'm wearily replanting all over again. The drought has not broken as the "long rains" failed – three years now. So, you are coming to a jolly place. Please let me know if there is anything I can do for you. *If* it is raining in Uganda as you approach here and the roads are bad, I'll drive over and pick you and *White Nile* up.

If you get to Kitale look up Frank and Tania Waldron (she's a *White Russian* out of Bronxville, N.Y.).

Also there is a hell of a nice little pub on the top of the airport at Khartoum – not open to transient air passengers but you could bull your way in.

At all events, I'll expect you here for Christmas anyway, and will pen up the turkey now.

The local Turkana put on one of a hell of a fine Ngona, and it's a pretty good holiday season in the neighborhood – if you can stand the pace. I have a horse, D.V., running in the Kenya Grand National on Boxing Day (day after C.) and there are all sorts of other fun and games – so don't "get caught in a pub" up country.

Keep me posted on your next address so I can be one jump ahead of you. Won't register this as might freeze it.

Cheers and God bless,

Sam S.

Give my love to those gorgeous popsies in Rome!!!

＊　　＊　　＊

JUNE 28

Back in Rome. Back on via Margutta, Pensione Forte, Taverna Margutta, back to blackened calves' brains near the Spanish Steps.

I opened up the machine on the autostrada, and we sailed down here in one day. God, she had power, which she delivered so gracefully, with hardly a murmur or complaint. We were now sporting flashy Italian red helmets with visors, black leather gloves handcrafted in Florence, and racing goggles. We have a windscreen but, at 80 mph, raindrops can sting like bees. In this hot summer weather we prefer to wear T-shirts, but have learned to cover up. Big bugs impact like meteorites, can put an unprotected eye out. We wear bandanas to protect lower face and neck. In the evening, after the long ride, I lovingly caressed our goddess and cleaned her of road and bug spatter.

We are planning to stay here a few days, indulge in a little more Italian food, wine, and culture before heading south toward the flaming Sahara. Now that we are launched, we feel no hurry.

Also to detain us in Rome: my mother, stepfather, and sister are staying at the Grand Hotel. They have crossed the Atlantic before we head off into the unknown to check that we are not totally nuts. They don't know where this adventure is taking us; nor do we. That is the deep-bedded passion of it.

JULY 2

Got dragged over the coals last night. Joe felt threatened by the seductive proximity of my family, whom he felt might contrive to put a stopper on our project. During dinner at the Grand my mother suggested that we escort sister Susie on a tour of Greece. Maybe she hoped we would all end up on some idyllic Aegean island rather than the Heart of Darkness. My sister wisely declined.

My mother had been in touch with Sam Small's brother George. She went to the Oldfields School in Maryland and they had friends in common. The fact that both Sam and George went to Princeton and were in Ivy finally seemed to legitimize this experience in her eyes. It is all getting a bit weird: our grand adventure is turning into a social occasion.

JULY 11, PENSIONE SULTANA, NAPLES

We missed the boat to Palermo, but we didn't mind. Maybe we'll stay here a few days more. Back to alley cats and laundry lines. There is no rush.

Vesuvio. We climbed it. Huge, ugly black lava sculptures. Ground hot near the top. We could feel the heat through our boots. Smoke or steam pouring out of fissures. Stink of sulfur. Amazing view of the bay. Our guide said that another eruption is due *any time now.* Like a pregnant woman, the old girl is overdue. We hurried back down and raced away on the machine.

Pliny the Younger chronicled the devastating Vesuvius eruption of AD 79. The first sign that something was up:

a narrow stem of smoke rising to a round plume above the mountain, which he compared to the outline of the umbrella pine, of which there are millions here. That simple description gives us a precise image of what that lethal cloud first looked like. Great literature – it instructs for centuries. This vivid description was contained in a letter to Marcus Aurelius. The point is: he wrote it all down!

JULY 18, HOTEL MARCO POLO, PALERMO

After garaging the machine, we walked through the city looking for a fish restaurant. In Lerici we ate a lot of fish and we wanted more. We love seafood, and don't expect to see much of it in the desert. Suddenly, a strong, brown, barefoot young man, naked to the waist, blue bandana wrapped around his head like a turban, trotted out of a side street with a huge silver fish over his shoulder.

We couldn't tell, in the twilight, whether it was a shark or a tuna but, whatever it was, it was a fish – big, shiny, and fresh-looking.

Joe: "Let's follow this guy. Let's see where he goes."

We followed. After a block or two, he dived into a restaurant with the catch over his shoulder.

We followed him in. A kind of dark, gloomy place where you imagine mafia men gather to make deals, decide who to rub out.

White tablecloths. The waiter brought the menu. Joe's hunch had been right: it was *all* fish. And we had it all: sea urchins, which Mario had taught us how to crack open and spoon out the orange roe; grilled swordfish, freshly sliced off the monster we had followed through the door; a liter of house white, espresso, and cigarettes.

It doesn't come much better than this. As we dined, the restaurant gradually filled. We were right: mafia types in brown suits muttering over shady deals; their wives in the corner sipping cocktails. Confident, flashy, but nervous. Worried their kids might get bumped off.

* * *

TUNISIA

JULY 19, GRAND HOTEL DE FRANCE, RUE MUSTAPHA MBAREK, TUNIS

There is a serious disturbance going on in this city. We don't know quite what. Gangs of young men surge through the streets, chanting slogans and throwing stones. Many shops are closed or boarded up. We have been told that French soldiers are shooting Tunisian men, women, and children. We don't know where or why.

Even I know, from my studies at Princeton, that the French pulled out of Tunisia in 1956. Habib Bourguiba was elected prime minister. He is very pro-French.

I thought the French had gone, but apparently the Foreign Legion have not. The city echoes with a frenzy of patriotism.

Otherwise there is little to report about this Arab–European city, except our satisfaction that we have finally set foot on African soil. We walked through the Kasbah, observed the graceful Muslim men in long robes and their veiled women. All fascinating, but I am only an outsider. Here, surrounded by chaos, confusion, and death, I better appreciate Camus' estimation of the 1905 Russian terrorists who gave their lives that something better might follow.

It is good to be with Joe, who has lit up and is beginning to exude the confidence he had in Lima. Once again, we are totally out of telephone contact with our families. Letters cannot track us because we have no fixed address. We have spent hours poring over maps and discussing what the next move will be. No one is looking over our shoulders; no one is criticizing. We have no one to guide us, but two heads are better than one. Best of all is the no telephone. Health-wise we are A-OK.

Hand-holding among men appeals to Joe strongly. Hmmm.

My father said I should participate in the affairs of my country, help it along some intelligent path, and not isolate myself in some foreign land. He was missing the point, as I am missing it. The point is to find a reason to live: how it is to be achieved is of secondary importance.

No, no, no. This is way too existential and in no way applies to me. I intend to go on exploring until I find the thing I am meant to do. It might come early or it might come late; the point is to not stop experimenting.

We are staying in a comfortable hotel on the edge of the Arab quarter. As usual the machine was mobbed; the Arabs have never seen anything like it (not since Rommel departed). We ended up parking her in the lobby. What is certain is that all Tunisians unanimously love Americans. Say you are an American and they applaud and offer their services. They are amazing at languages and speak enough English, French, or Italian, so we can get along. Veiled women shoot provocative glances from hyper-expressive eyes.

JULY 20

Not feeling so well — *mal de stomach.* Living on Coca-Cola. Went and bought an Arab "*saq*" in the souk. Beautiful, white, handmade, all for 1½ dinar ($3).

Camus' *Rebel* making a deep impression. Perhaps the most enlightened piece of literature I have read. A brilliant sequel to *The Stranger*, *La Peste*, *Caligula*, the short stories, etc. What a man! What a mind! And to think that not much more than a year ago, Jan. 4, 1960 I think it was, word circulated in the Princeton ice hockey locker room, at Baker rink, where we were dressing for the game, that Albert Camus had been killed in a car crash in France. Forty-seven years old, Nobel Prize in literature, and I didn't even know who he was!

Joe: he opened my eyes.

Back to the war: we are having a small one in Tunisia. We were inside the British embassy, waiting for our visas to Uganda and Kenya, when a mob ran past on the street. Rocks started smashing through the windows. We took cover beneath a heavy wooden table, the dining-room table, I think it was, when whom should I bump heads with beneath the mahogany but Prof. Manfred Halpern, my tutor at Princeton! An expert on Middle Eastern politics, he had just driven from Cairo to Tunis, following the exact same route we were planning to take, but from the opposite direction.

Later we sipped mint tea in a café. This is the situation as he explained it:

Thirty miles north of Tunis, at the naval base of Bizerte, the French and the Tunisians are shooting it out. There is little evidence of this in Tunis, except for shops closed in protest, radios blaring marching music, speeches by Bourguiba, and truckloads of volunteers off to battle. The Tunisians worship their leader, and have even composed songs in his name.

As the Moroccans had quite easily managed to get France to quit their bases, Bourguiba is under pressure to do the same. He has been quietly negotiating for the past two years. He wants to be the leader of a North African federation and has to take the initiative. Thus he issued an ultimatum to President Charles de Gaulle that the French leave Bizerte immediately, or the town and base would be blockaded by land. The note also demanded that Tunisia share some of the Algerian Sahara that the French had reserved for themselves and are now occupying in a series of outposts. (The border between the two countries has never been formalized.) As Tunisia is small and without oil, it would be to its advantage to have some extra space with oil potential. With Algeria verging on independence after a long and bloody rebellion, it would be easier for Tunisia to get new land from the French than from an independent Algeria, which Bourguiba hopes to lead in a future federation.

De Gaulle's reply was that the French would meet force with force. Bourguiba called up unarmed volunteers to blockade all roads into Bizerte. This civilian force (many had brought along their wives and children, as though it were a picnic) was cut down by Foreign Legion machine guns, and bombarded by French tanks and planes. The massacre continued as the French bombed the town of Bizerte and demanded the whole area in order to protect their sovereign rights.

In protest against the barbarity the shops of Tunis were closed. I now better understand the plaintive, sometimes frantic outcry against colonialism from delegates of the newly emerged African countries at the U.N. The matter of Bizerte has been taken before the U.N. by Monsieur Slim of Tunisia. Prof. Halpern thought that by now a ceasefire might have already been called.

Prof. Halpern informed us that an International Youth Conference was taking place in Tunis. What with my background in African and Middle Eastern politics, he urged me to attend.

What alarmed Joe and me most of all was Prof. Halpern's warning that the American Sixth Fleet might arrive any minute to extract *all* Americans from Tunisia. *Tout de suite!*

JULY 21, HOTEL SPLENDID,*
KAIROUAN, 9 P.M.

We wanted to stay longer in Tunis. We had planned to visit the ruins at Carthage, but Prof. Halpern's warning (that's the way we interpreted it) that the U.S. Sixth Fleet might evacuate all Americans threw us into a minor panic. The last thing we want is to be taken back to Naples on a battleship, never to see the African shore again. Forget Carthage. Forget the Youth Conference. We packed up, gassed up, and headed out of town.

KAIROUAN, 4 A.M.

(Too hot to sleep, I am writing by flashlight.) In Tunis the climate was moderated by a bubble of moist air puffed up by the Med. But go ten miles inland, and you're in a furnace.

The wailing voice of the muezzin (in fact multiple muezzins, near and far; their high-pitched songs trail over this many-domed city) sound like voices of the dead complaining to one another. Tremendously weird. Somehow soothing. Today, or yesterday, we got our first taste of the eloquent African landscape: an arid lushness that produces citrus and dates. Rows of olive trees run to the horizon. This

* = excellent

was once the breadbasket for Rome. We raced along an avenue of huge century plants in bloom. The collapsing plants had pushed up phallic stalks as stiff and as tall as telephone poles. The setting sun ribbed the road with their shadows.

We are heading into the unknown, with all of Africa before us.

One thing the French know how to do is to build roads. Flat, graded, and invariably smooth, they make life exhilarating aboard the speeding machine. Bugs as big as walnuts bounced off the windscreen. Locusts, I think they were. We kept gloves and goggles on and sleeves rolled down to fend off the critters. To get hit by one of them at 80 mph could knock you off the machine.

Kairouan rises up from the dull brown plain in a series of minarets, girdled by date palms, that preside over a tumble of low, geometric buildings. At once you sense there is something extraordinary about this city. It ranks second, third, or fourth in holiness after Mecca, with the old traditions preserved. This was our first encounter with spiritual architecture in Africa. All women veiled, with some faces completely hidden. They passed by like ghosts. Affection among men much in evidence. You see men holding hands, even kissing. It seems natural here and Joe approves; me – I'm not so sure.

Men wear light summer burnooses elegantly, loosely, like togas. At night no women in the streets. We visited the great mosque – Djmaa al-Kebir. Old men nodded, silently saluting us as they came out. We peered into the great pillared courtyard. Three hundred marble pillars pilfered from Roman and Byzantine ruins.

JULY 22, KAIROUAN

Now we are wearing robes, more comfortable and cool than close-fitting Western dress. The Kairouanis very friendly. Wherever we go they greet us with smiles and nods. Already we salute many people. Everybody in town knows us. The machine draws a crowd, like we arrived by spaceship.

What is certain is that all Tunisians love America. What we did to merit such affection I do not know.

All these observations must be treated as being strictly superficial. It is very difficult, at least so soon, to have any insight into the Muslim world, or to understand anything about it. The position of women seems very low. They may rule at home, but the streets belong to men. The people may be poor, but they are invariably graceful and welcoming. Like a *buenos días* to an Indian in Peru, here a simple *bonjour* brings forth a smile and good feeling. The friendliest people in the world make their homes in poor countries. That's what I learned in Peru.

I bought two beautiful hand-woven carpets and mailed them home. Every night Joe counts his remaining T-checks.

The world has caught up with our dream, doused cold water all over it. They were bringing the dead back from Bizerte. The sorrow and the wailing! The funerals of Tunisians killed on their own soil by foreigners brought home the oppression and injustice that a colonial power can inflict on defenseless people in underdeveloped countries.

The pain these people suffered because of the pride of a foreign army. This is the army of a nation that condemned the Soviet suppression of the Hungarian uprising of 1956. Bizerte underlined the ironic nature of the world we live in, a world where blame and abuse are thrown about by those equally guilty. The Tunisians, pacific and docile, could not fight against the French army, one of the most powerful in the world. This small and weak nation had to depend on the goodwill of the strong – the U.S. The result was slaughter. I'll never forget it.

(All these notes scribbled by flashlight, notebook on my knees.) In these darkened alleys (always a distant light), with everyone around me grieving for the young men lost at Bizerte, I feel a strange, bitter elation.

JULY 23, HOTEL NOUVEL, GAFSA

After two nights and a day in the holy city of Kairouan we have come to this oasis town on the edge of the desert. This is the old Roman town of Capsa. Along the way we passed many Roman ruins – impressive in their nakedness against the desert and sky, whispering of days when North Africa was much less desiccated than it is today. Tunisia supplied Rome with wheat, olives and olive oil, dates, citrus, and wild animals. In Gafsa, the Roman baths were still in use, and we went swimming with swarms of Arab boys. They dove off rooftops and splashed around like shiny brown seals.

All these elements lead me to conclude that life in Tunisia is actually not all that different from what it was like in Roman times. People still dress the same – in sensible, light, voluminous robes that wrap you in a comfortable bubble of body warmth, repelling extremes of hot and cold. They still do the same things – gather olives, citrus, and dates for export. The climate, which has not much changed, dictates the way people lead their lives. One big difference: in those days the people owed their allegiance to Rome; now it's Mecca.

HOTEL ESSAADA, TOZEUR

The heat (120°)† is really getting to us. So far the roads are good and the machine is running well. Difficult to sleep because of the heat. You just lie there, naked in a puddle of your own sweat, listening to the dogs that talk all night. But that is the hour when I get my writing done.

Khubz, khubz = bread, bread. In Tunisian the word for bark is the same as for bread.

At 4 a.m. we set out for Tozeur over 50 miles of incredibly uncomfortable washboard road, with sand dunes spilling across. Considerable difficulty in negotiating the machine through sand. The heat immense. The *White Nile* overheated, freezing the throttle at 60 km/h. But we finally made it.

Tozeur must be one of the hottest places in the world. The week before, we were told, the temperature in the sun pushed 150°! Impossible to drive water-cooled cars. Hence the omnipresence of the French air-cooled 2CV. The air, however, is extremely dry, humidity practically nil. It is possible, therefore, to be fairly comfortable in the shade of a palm tree, even when the temperature out in the desert is up near boiling!

TOZEUR

A classic Saharan oasis where forests of date palms sprout from sand moistened by underground water. A magical sight, but so hot we ate the equivalent of one small meal per day (in the evening), but drank gallons of water (bottled), Coke, lemonade, beer – anything wet and cool. We had a continual

---

† The highest recorded temperatures on planet earth are 136°F (Sahara) and 135°F (Death Valley).

craving for drink. We never ceased to be thirsty. The more you drink the more you want. Impossible to do anything during the day but wait for the sun to go down.

Nevertheless, at 4 p.m. we jumped on the machine (throttle now unstuck) and pushed on to Nefta, an even larger oasis near the border with Algeria. The road good, but at 70 mph the wind oven-hot.

The road bordered the Great Salt Desert, 5,000 sq. km., known as the Chott el Djerid, or Locust Leg, which stretched to the horizon, ghostly white and eerily shimmering in the heat. One of the most terrifying sights I have ever seen. Death on a platter. We had originally planned to cross this vast salt pan to Kebili, but were told you can break through the crust and sink into the quicksand beneath.

A month earlier a French couple set out in their Deux Chevaux and were never seen again. Apparently the vehicle, when it didn't turn up in Kebili, was tracked by the authorities, who located the place where it had been swallowed by the salt pan. Not one trace of the car or its occupants remained. Drowned in one big hungry slurp of mud, salt, and sand.

Nefta is a magnificent oasis, as exotic as you can imagine. We wandered through the forest of date palms, nibbling dates, figs, peaches – offered by friendly local farmers. We also went swimming! Not too refreshing. H_2O about 90°.

The people in Nefta, especially the young men, are less friendly. We were near the border with Algeria, where a war is still going on. Rebels about. These strange-looking people (men only, the women totally veiled) are the descendants of the Vandals, a German tribe that migrated from the Baltic via France, Spain, and Morocco to Carthage (Tunis) (c. fifth century AD) to harass the Romans, leaving behind a trail of blue eyes. Blue eyes, blond hair, red hair which, combined with tawny African skin, make for exotic faces, sometimes bizarre. We drove back to Tozeur, passing herds of camels along the way. The greatest road danger was that all sorts of animals – camels, goats, dogs, etc. – were continually wandering across it. Plus people sound asleep on the tar. When we got back to Tozeur the town was just waking up from its day-long nap.

HOTEL DAR FAIZA, THE ISLAND OF DJERBA. 8 P.M.

Way too hot to sleep, but the air fresh at 4:40 a.m., when we were up and off back toward the coast fleeing the oppressive heat, via Gafsa and Gabes to this fabled island.

We kicked the machine to life at dawn, and set off across sand and among palms, with the cool air and clear view producing a feeling of freedom, perfect soaring freedom. I don't know its equal. Not that kind. One hot sweet coffee and a sugar doughnut to keep us going the whole day. We carried four one-liter bottles of H_2O in case we broke down. We always covered up – hat or helmet. It would be no joke to get stuck out there. Virtually no dawn traffic on the smooth, flat, well-made road. After we got past the washboard, I just opened her up and we flew across Tunisia.

This, apparently, was the fabled island of the Lotus Eaters, or Lotophagi, where Odysseus' crew, on their ten-year-voyage to get home to Ithaka from Troy, an adventure that took them all over the Med, was seduced by consuming this mysterious plant. They forgot their friends; they didn't want to go home. My Greek and Latin studies come in handy while traveling across these classical lands. I can read some inscriptions, but what the lotus was I do not know. A water lily. My copy of Herodotus' *The Histories* tells me the lotus fruit was as sweet as a date. Maybe it was the dates. Date palms grow in their millions here. Maybe the dates were stuffed with hashish by the canny locals. Or maybe Odysseus' crew, like us, were having the time of their lives and didn't want the adventure to end.

JULY 26, DJERBA, 11:30 P.M.

Gide and Flaubert visited this island. And many other writers. Now me. Nothing but sand and palm groves: the strange-looking white-domed houses and mosques date from another world. A full moon so bright you could read the newspaper out of doors. We sleep outside; the sea breeze a blessed relief from the crushing heat of the interior. The dogs talked all night – *khubz, khubz*. The still, clear night rings with the call from the mosque – softer and more melodious than the voice in Kairouan. A young boy's voice. In Tunis it sounded like a call to war. I write by candlelight, with a candle stuck in the sand.

The market of the major town of Houmpt-Souk was a merry madhouse. We have learned, when possible, to breakfast at the market, breakfast consisting of a carefully selected melon and strong black coffee. Here we breakfast on *brik*, a pastry concoction with a fragile egg inside. The trick is to bite into the middle, suck out the warm liquid yolk, and chew up the crust.

The national dish of Tunisia is couscous (semolina) plus a choice of meat – lamb or goat – with vegetables and gravy, which is tasty but indigestible if you drink anything with it. Liquid expands the semolina in your stomach, and you feel like you've swallowed a football. In this heat we don't eat much. We prefer to eat fresh fish. There is plenty here, plus squid. The Jewish community produces a local hooch: fig eau de vie.

Flat stretches of palms on sand. Beaches contract and expand hundreds of yards with the tide. Old bearded Jews in djellabas and skullcaps huddle in the shade of a white wall. Birds flit through the 2,500-yr.-old synagogue. The Kaddish still sung in Jewish villages. Tribes of lemon-eyed, broad-nosed people. Turkish fort, rose in the morning sun, human shit clotting the battlements, turning back into the soil. Everybody has been here. Odysseus, Hannibal, Romans, Arabs, Turks, French, Rommel, Montgomery. Now us.

Arab boys hang around like jackals, waiting for a sign.

The people friendly, more friendly than in the desert. Colors: blue and white. Dhows banked on the horizon. Sand, smell of the sea, the harbor. Squid and freshly caught sponges drying on the same line with the laundry. Lateen-rigged fishing boats stranded on the beach by the receding tide. Small boys and an old woman wade out among them looking for clams in the slimy, ankle-deep water. Seaweed rolling in the shadow of the port. Plumed trees above the shimmering, quicksilver mirage. Smell of rotten sponges. An old, one-legged fisherman is sprawled in the courtyard, keeping an eye on his sponges on the line. The stamping of mules. In Djerba time stopped a long time ago.

* * *

LIBYA

JULY 29, 1961, HOTEL EXCELSIOR, TRIPOLI

There may not be enough pages left in this notebook for me to describe what happened to us today. We were lucky – incredibly lucky – Joe lucky to be alive. We are both horribly sunburned from an entire day in the desert. Me worse than Joe. He is darker complected and has a mop of thick, curly, brown–black hair. The backs of my hands look like under-done barbecue: red and raw, with fingernails black with oil, grease, and desert dirt.

The hotel shower let down a few squirts. I took the thing apart and with the awl of my Swiss knife reamed the lime-scale from the little holes, and we had a hearty flow. No way to describe the relief.

It was a bad day from the start. We set out from Djerba at 5 a.m. but ran out of gas. We pushed the machine a mile into Medenine, where we tanked up, breakfasted, and headed south. It was noon before we reached the Tunisian border post at Ben Gardane. The heat was intense, with mirages everywhere, the horizon jumping. Like a wall of mirrors, the mirages house you in on all sides except from windward, where a sneaky little breeze leaking in opens the door a crack.

The friendly Tunisian customs official stamped our passports and asked if we had a Carnet de Passage for Libya. This document guarantees you will not sell your vehicle in the country you are entering. We said no: in Tunis it was impossible to obtain this document for the motorcycle with its special oval German "Z" export plate. At the Libyan embassy, where we got our visas, we were assured that we could enter the country without it.

The Tunisian guard said no. They won't let you in.

We had no choice but to press on into the desolation that is Libya. In Tunisia we had passed palm trees and animals; but in Libya there is nothing. The flat, pebbly plain stretched to the horizon, with crescent-shaped dunes perched here and there, oddly soft-looking, like pillows. Ideal terrain for tank battles; not much else.

I wonder now if that desert sun didn't addle our brains. The risks we were about to take. The recklessness of our decisions, with never a thought for the peril we were putting ourselves in. We both could have been killed – not once but *twice*.

Mirages and the choking heat: we hoped we were doing the right thing. We hadn't passed another vehicle for miles. We prayed our faithful machine would see us through.

A strip of no-man's-land separates the Tunisian and Libyan frontier posts, about 20 miles apart. At the Libyan side we approached a bar across the road, like a RR crossing. We eased up, got off the machine, and propped her on the side stand as a soldier carrying a rifle ambled from a shack.

We handed over our passports with the Libyan visas. The language of communication switched from French to Italian. He examined the passports and asked for the Carnet de Passage. We said we didn't have one. He shrugged his shoulders and said he couldn't let us in without it. All this in the shimmering desert and about 120° heat. We told him the people at his embassy in Tunis said we didn't need it. No, he said. We must go back and get it. Back. Five hundred miles back to Tunis in that heat for a piece of paper. To show his goodwill he gave us each a glass of water.

We drove back two or three miles, got off the machine and unfolded the map. It looked as though the road we were on was about five miles from the sea. In Djerba we had noticed that the tide went far out, leaving a wide, flat, hard-packed beach that kids rode their bikes on. If we could reach that beach, maybe we could drive along it a few miles, than duck back to the hard road behind the police post and head toward Tripoli. We had our visas, but the machine did not. There was no way we were going back to Tunis. Not in that heat.

The main problem was sand: big dunes north of the road between us and the sea. We would have to find a way through. We had already learned what an effort it takes to push a two-wheeled machine through sand. Rommel knew better: his Afrika Korps brought three-wheeled BMWs to Africa.

We started out. It was hell. To get over a dune was impossible; we had to go around. The basins enclosed by the twin horns of those crescent-shaped dunes collected the heat. They were like ovens. The heat was burning through the soles of our boots. The beautiful dunes became the enemy. You soon lost your sense of direction. After a mile or so we realized we didn't know if we were going north, south, east, or west. Weaving among dunes too high to see over, we became disoriented. All we had was our track back, which that evil little wind was quietly erasing. But this particular anxiety was replaced by a worse, much worse menace.

We were suddenly surrounded by armed men who had materialized from nowhere among the dunes. Gray-beards and tough-looking leathery individuals in ragged djellabas. About eight of them. They were carrying an assortment of primitive weapons: an antique rifle, a revolver, curved swords, clubs, and, most charming of all, a pickax. A posse of vigilantes, apparently, their hatred of foreigners fired by the atrocities at Bizerte. We both immediately realized that we were in an extremely dangerous situation. One false word or move and they could kill us, bury us in the sand, and nobody would ever know what happened. Our families would never learn the truth. Disappeared. Covered by the sands of Africa. Lost and gone, forever, without a trace. No witnesses. The machine would survive. They wouldn't bury that. That was their prize. And the only clue.

One of them spoke a little French, which meant they were Tunisian, not Libyan. I didn't know whether that was good or bad: probably bad. Their blood was hot; they were in the hunt for the European killers of their children.

"Who are you and where are you going?"

I did the talking.

"We're American, and we're going to the beach."

That response, in retrospect, had to be one of the most frivolous in history. Guns cocked and pointed at us, swords and clubs raised and poised to strike, and all we're doing is going to the beach.

But there was a magic word: "*Mirikani, mirikani,*" was whispered among them. The weapons dropped a few inches.

We dug out our passports and handed them over. I pointed out the words "The United States of America" to the one who seemed able to read. The passports were handed from one to the other. Everyone had to have a look.

"*Mirikani, mirikani.*"

I believe now, and will for the rest of my life, that had we been French and had French passports, that band of vigilantes would have murdered us on the spot, and with perfect justification. Tunisian soldiers and civilians are being gunned down by the Foreign Legion in Bizerte. All over the country people are grieving for young men dead. This would be one small act of revenge.

"*Mirikani, mirikani.*" As though we were men from Mars.

The passports were handed back.

"Go back to the road."

Which we did. That evil little breeze, whose sole intention seemed to be to lose us in the middle of nowhere, had left few tracks for us to retrace our route. We didn't have a clue where we were. The Tunisians showed the way. In the end it might be said that they saved our lives.

We were mighty relieved to get back to the tar. It was cooler than those superheated basins among the dunes. But the heat was no longer a problem; we were almost used to it. It was now 3 p.m. and still about 120°.

What were we going to do?

"Let's run it."

My Confederate compadre is absolutely fearless. If he needs to do something, he does it, whatever the difficulties; if he wants to go somewhere, he goes, whatever the obstacles. He just charges through.

We had both noticed, on our brief visit to the Libyan border post, that the bar across the road left a gap on the left, about a yard wide, for walkers and their animals to pass. I figured we could squeeze through, but with one proviso.

"I'm driving. If there's any lead in the air, you can soak it up."

"Get going! I'm burning up. Let's run the border!"

So we eased up to the Libyan control post once more, 10 mph, like we were going to get off and talk it all over again. The soldier and his gun came out of the shack. I had the thought: why the hell don't we just bribe the guy? $10 and we'd be in Tripoli by now.

But the die was cast. Our fate was already sealed. I maneuvered the machine through the gap and hit the gas.

To our absolute horror, at that very instant a Libyan patrol vehicle, bristling with guns and soldiers, steamed out of the desert. With a war cry they took off after us.

"Gun it!"

I didn't need to be told. We were already in fourth and accelerating through 80 on another smooth, flat road, this one made by Rommel and/or Montgomery. We heard a few pops from behind. We both lay low over the machine to reduce our target profile.

Within a minute or so I thought we had outpaced the Libyan vehicle with so much smoke pouring out of the radiator it looked like it was steam-driven. We sat up as the machine purred across the desert. This was more like it. God bless German engineers! We had left hell behind and were headed toward heaven. But our euphoria didn't last long.

Joe grunted and slumped heavily against my back. "Oh, shit!"

I yelled, "What's wrong?"

"Keep going!"

After about 30 miles we had to stop at the town of Zuwarah. Boulders had been rolled across the road. Palm logs. And dozens of people. More running every minute. Soldiers with guns. The patrol vehicle had radioed ahead: a roadblock had been set up.

We stopped the machine and got off. To my astonishment, Joe and I were stuck together. By his blood. We didn't say a word; we just pulled apart. My T-shirt ripped from his. The patrol vehicle roared up to applause and shouts. The soldiers jumped down and pointed their rifles. If we hadn't been so scared, we could have been celebrities, such was the excitement in the crowd.

Joe was bleeding profusely from a gunshot wound that creased his right shoulder near the base of his neck. Had it been an inch to the left he would have been a dead man.

Nuns were summoned. They came with hats like seagulls sailing. They took Joe away and sewed him up. No anesthetic. He joined me in the cell. Zuwarah was a prison town. Out the window I monitored the urchins milling around the machine. I had the key in my pocket.

About an hour later the bars opened and in stepped a Libyan officer, about our age, immaculate in starched khaki and green beret.

"Now, what's it all about, boys?"

Perfect English.

We showed him our passports. The Egyptian, Sudanese, and B.E.A. visas must have convinced him we weren't planning to spend the rest of our lives in Libya.

He ordered mint tea and pistachio sweets. The tea was served by prisoners who were wandering all over the place. Every time we looked at them they roared with laughter. Thus, we all ended up laughing our heads off. It was a crazy experience, and I'm sure the border patrol will tell their children about it.

It's hard to describe the lift their tea gives. The requisite three glasses. A pure sugar high.

Since that glass of water at the Libyan post we hadn't drunk or eaten anything all day. We chatted about the U.S. and Libya: how a poor Muslim state and a rich Christian one could learn from each other. How we could join forces and rule the world. No communists allowed. He had studied at an English university. He was correct, polite, and welcoming. It's amazing how, in Africa, complete strangers can make you feel at home. Those warriors in the dunes included. They set out to murder us but ended up saving our lives. In Africa you feel you are learning something new every day. About people, especially poor people; humanity, not humanities. Something that got left off the curriculum at Princeton.

He stamped our passports, giving us 14 days to cross the country.

Heck, we can handle that: it is only about 1,000 miles to Egypt, with about 20 historic sites to visit along the way.

We changed into clean shirts. The men from Mars boarded the gleaming machine. Thankfully, the urchins had left it alone. The whole town gave us a rapturous send-off. Best time they'd had in their lives. Ours too, in a way. The soldiers who had pointed their rifles at us a few hours earlier now fired them into the air. We shook hands all around. All friends now, united to rule the world. Two hours later we were in Tripoli.

HOTEL EXCELSIOR, TRIPOLI

The voice of Mel Allen, of the N.Y. Yankees, was broadcast over the radio via Wheelus (Strategic Air Command) Air Force Base (the largest in the world) outside Tripoli:

"Going... going... gone!" Mickey Mantle had just hit another home run. He was going for Babe Ruth's record. Now came the ad for White Owl cigars... surreal.

Our shirts are soaking in a sink full of pink water. Another casualty is my face, which was almost destroyed by the sun and wind off the desert. It is now undergoing treatment with Johnson's First Aid Cream. Joe is chewing aspirins to kill the pain.

When I think now of what very nearly happened... why didn't we just bribe the guy?

LEPTIS MAGNA

We spent a magical two days and even more magical two nights in that ancient Roman seaport, birthplace of Septimius Severus, the first and only Africa-born emperor. He spoke the Latin tongue with a Punic accent and died in York in 211.

It was once a city of 60,000, but we had the place to ourselves. Miraculously preserved and wonderfully pure in form, the contrast of the marble theater, temples, baths, forum, and basilica against a sea of a thousand hues, ranging from the lightest blue to the deepest purple, is breathtaking. The architecture and city planning, with broad streets lined with marble benches and marble statues, blends harmoniously with sea and desert. The baths: ten pools of hot and cold waters. Gymnasiums, *palestrae*, toilets, and Turkish baths. The forum gigantic and the basilica almost perfectly preserved. They say the city is much looted, but you'd never know it. Those who watched performances in the huge theater must have been distracted by spectacular views of sea and sky. This pride of the Empire inspired many emperors to embellish.

The fishing port is silted in, but on the marble counters

along its rim you can make out the grooves where the fish-mongers sharpened their knives. The old lighthouse still sits out on the tip of the breakwater. One must not forget that in those times North Africa was not the desert it is today, but the chief granary for Rome. Elephants and other wild animals were captured and shipped north for the Games. The wild-animal business was huge, with tentacles stretching all over Africa.

I should have written that Joe, I, Ali and Fatimah, and their three girls had the place to ourselves. They lived in an improvised stone and palm-frond shack propped up against the theater wall. Aisha (seven), Kinza (five), and Batoul (two): three brown-skinned beauties. What a life they lead: their purity among the purity of the statues. Leptis is their playground. They had the whole city to themselves. Fatima grilled the sardines that Ali had caught in the morning. Tomato, pepper, and onion salad from their garden, the incredibly reviving green Libyan tea, and the fig eau de vie from Djerba. Fatima gave us sacks stuffed with straw to sleep on. Morning: eggs from their chickens, barley bread from a wood-fired oven. All for about $5. Including their welcoming cheerful selves. Lovely curious children whom we took for rides among the ruins.

Here is one experience which will stick, even without this record. Moonlit walks among stately columns whispering of a vanished empire. Joe was in his element: classical times, nourishing democracy and literature, esp. the theater, fine art, and architecture, an era when men loved men, without shame or guilt.

To have masters in village schools
To teach 'em classics not hogwash.

EZRA POUND

AUGUST 2, MISRATAH

(With the sea, sand, and sky so big, the road so long, I'm not exactly sure where we are.)

Big sand. Treacherous tongues slither across the road. If you don't hit the brakes in time, you could flip. All day on the machine – 600 km – culminating in a relaxing and enjoyable tea with hooded Libyans at a road station where wind, sand, darkness, and contaminated gasoline detained us. And, yes, there were moments that can never be forgotten. We screamed into the wind our joy of being in Africa. The magnificent countryside whipping past: desert stretching to infinity on the right, the sea horizon (Gulf of Sirte) of a million blue hues to the left. When the heat became intolerable, we pulled her up, propped her up, got off, and ran into the sea.

N.B. This desert is not to be toyed with. Mile after mile, trashed by the armies of Rommel and Montgomery, thousands of oil drums, the occasional charred skeleton of a truck or armored car, a piece of plane wreckage. And the whole place is mined: every day, the locals say, half a dozen camels have their legs blown off.

Libya's major industry used to be the recovery and sale of scrap metal left behind by the war.

However, when the road is long, the journey tedious, fatigue creeps in. My warmth for Joe, I fear, succumbs to impatience and selfishness. But my respect for him I never doubt. We sat on a sand dune by the side of the road and discussed what we were reading. Here, on the road to Alexandria, it is *The Alexandria Quartet*. And, of course, Cavafy:

When you set out for Ithaka,
Ask that your way be long,
Full of adventure, full of instruction.

The big question (among many others) is: *how to use these experiences*? Presumably they will strengthen convictions, beliefs, character, etc., but where is this adventure taking us? The State Dept.? (No.) A life in agriculture? (Out.) In or out of society? (Which society?) We have no clear idea where it is taking us. What is clear is that it isn't taking us back home. I have no fixed address now, don't want one, don't need one. We are floating. The thought of returning to my former life in the U.S. seems an alien concept. Out of the question. Nostalgia for home has vamoosed.

We have tasted the lotus and we're not going back.

Not that I love my family and friends any less – it is that I am no longer capable of rejoining that oh-so-familiar life. A life full and free is what Joe said he wants. Emphasis drained from preoccupation with occupation; the important thing is how, where, and why to *live*. Whatever, I feel a strong urge to create – God, I must! But how? Where are the answers? Perhaps, now, only the questions matter. If I miss the essence of that experience, or fail to perceive it, I feel that through this diary I am preserving some of it, which could be reviewed later. These pages add some form to the formless life we are leading; a bit of daily discipline to prop me up. The easy thing about a diary is that you don't have to make anything up; you just record this piece of your life as you go along.

We were in another roadside police station – stopped by wind, sand, and reports of heavy sandstorms ahead – in the middle of nowhere, an old Italian rest house. Joe: Italian architecture in Libya is fascist crap; Mussolini's Italy produced nothing but a RR timetable. Maybe not even that. But we were dead tired and thankful for Spanish rice and Libyan tea, which gave a heady lift.

As in Tunisia, the Libyan national drink is sugary mint tea, with the requisite three glasses served from the same pot. In Tunisia they call the first glass *fort comme la mort* ("strong as death"), the second *douce comme la vie* ("sweet like life"), and the third *sucrée comme l'amour* ("honeyed with love").

I had a chat with an old Arab who spoke Italian. Elegant, graceful, old-fashioned hospitality. We took off our boots and sat on the mat. By custom, as guests, we ate before anyone else. We have learned to eat with the right hand only, reserving the left for ablutions. We spent the night on the same mat with our new-found friends and were off at dawn – straight into the blazing sunrise.

AUGUST 3/4

Benghazi: an oil town – only behind Caracas, Venezuela, in expense.

Joe has been feeling under the weather with blood poisoning from his wound. This actually turned out to be a stroke of luck, because when we appeared at the Seventh Day Adventist Mission Hospital, they offered to put us *both* up, free of charge. Joe got an armful of antibiotics, while I enjoyed the clean sheets, the food (vegetarian), and hospital services.

The Seventh Day Adventists (despite their kindness and hospitality) give one a creepy feeling of individuals confined to a limited realm of prejudices and beliefs that allows little or no scope beyond the accepted ideological framework.

German med students – a good sort. No meandering through Libya looking for the truth. They have done a good and thorough job collecting bugs.

Catch of the day: the wolf spider. (Tarantula.) Scorpions, both orange and black (Princeton colors). The black ones smaller but more venomous. Plus every sort of ant, locust, beetle, fly, mosquito. But no bees. No bees? No bees because in the Sahara there are no flowers. Wasps yes. But no bees.

Heck, we've seen flowers – orange and yellow sand poppies, growing on the beach.

Here the beach is 2,000 miles wide and 1,000 miles deep.

And we've seen Montgomery's Desert Rats – gerbils – hopping about.

AUGUST 4, THE HOTEL (THE ONLY ONE), HOTEL EXCELSIOR

In Cyrene the hillside ruins reminded Joe (and me somewhat) of Machu Picchu, with vistas stretching across plateaux–plains to the bluffs, the sea, the end of the earth. However, the Greek–Roman–Byzantine–Arab mishmash leaves no clear picture of what anything looked like. Cf. the architectural purity of Roman Leptis Magna.

My birthday. On its eve I feel, for the first time in my life, a kind of glory. Glory gained from this experience of living, and *humility* (another one of Joe's trigger words, endlessly repeated) for our good fortune to be able to do what we are doing. This sense of wonder is telling me something. The stagnation of "observing Tunisia" has lifted. Now we are "in it." There is no going back.

Cyrene (and its ancient port, Apollonia) is situated in the Libyan highlands, or "alps" as they are known. Here the air is relatively fresh and cool, a welcome change from the inferno that is the desert. This was once a large Greek colony, not unlike Paestum in southern Italy, not that far away across the water. The Greek city states expanded aggressively. The archaeological sites are impressive, but lack the architectural purity of Leptis. Layers of Greek, Roman, early Christian, and Byzantine civilizations, piled on top of one another, baffle the visitor.

When those entrepreneurial seafarers got blown off course, they simply started up a colony wherever they landed.

The view from the high plateau overlooking the sea: Joe and I sat among pillars at dusk, sipping cold beer and feeling we are in some sort of time warp, i.e. heaven.

Cyrene, wrote Herodotus, was named in honor of the mythological maiden Kurane, whose favorite sport was to throttle lions barehanded. Must have been quite a girl. Apollo was so impressed he carried her off to Libya (presumably to watch her strangle more lions).

AUGUST 5, HOTEL BRISTOL, TOBRUK

Twenty-three today. A year ago I was at the Univ. of Madrid, boning up on Spanish. I wonder where I'll be in another year – probably in a place not much different than this one.

This "inland sea" (*med + terra*) lay at the heart of the Roman Empire. It made the Empire possible. All the main countries front it, with Italy in the middle. Greece, Asia Minor, and Persia to the E; France and Spain to the W; and all of Africa, from Egypt to Morocco, to the S. Distances could be measured in hundreds, not thousands, of miles. We know about her legions and the roads they built, but Rome was fundamentally a naval power. Her fleet kept open the trade routes to the Empire, and the Empire made Rome rich.

Tobruk: not a bad town, pretty dull, noted primarily for its WWII cemeteries and battle monuments. Completely isolated by desert and sea, it makes you feel you are standing on the edge of the earth. A mystery why the British thought it so strategic. The harbor. Riding into town, we pulled up next to a Land Rover flying the Union Jack, where some soldiers were loading boxes. We said hello. They did not respond. They were speaking a language we did not understand.

The sergeant stepped forward.

"What can I do for you Yanks?"

"Nothing. We just wanted to say hello."

"Well, hello. We're busy here."

They must have been soldiers from a Welsh or Scottish regiment. Amazing how they have preserved their Celtic tongue. And not at all friendly.

El Alamein:

Nothing but ugly (stony, bumpy) desert marked by massive gloomy German and Italian war monuments and a vast British cemetery. Thousands died fighting over a scrap of uninhabitable desert. It showed how close Rommel came to taking the Canal.

My blond hair. The machine. Maybe those Scots in Tobruk thought we were Krauts.

* * *

EGYPT

AUGUST 6, 1961, SOLLUM

We approached the border uncertain about Egyptian requirements for the Carnet de Passage, although we had been assured by their embassy in Tripoli there would be no problem.

The Egyptian border guards greeted us with watermelon, bread, cheese, and onions, and never asked about the machine. Hey, the life of a border guard can be fun! One vehicle per month, and it's party time! We spent the night in that beautiful spot surrounded by high desert bluffs and entertained by the local barber. He had cut hair in Brooklyn and spoke some English.

AUGUST 7/8

Piccadilly Hotel, Alexandria, where we spent four hours in customs to get a permit for the machine: $25, which, I was assured, would be refunded when we leave Egypt.

Alexandria is a far cry from the burg described by Durrell. Now it is ugly, filthy, filled with thieves from the age of five to 60 who are always assailing us, swarming around like a pack of eels. In Egypt it's a lifetime occupation. The first morning I surprised a group of them attempting to dismantle the machine, with a policeman standing not 20 yards away, back turned. Luckily, nothing came off.

Before the war, with the British and French in control, this was a cosmopolitan and sophisticated city. The embassies had their summer residences here. Since the popular revolution of July 26, 1952, however, everything has become monochromatically Egyptian: the den of iniquity of the Middle East.

*   *   *

S. Small — Impala Farm
P.O. Box 92, Nanyuki

John Hopkins, Esq.
c/o The American Express,
Cairo,
Egypt.
August 4, 1961

Dear John and Partner,

Your card from Tunisia arrived a couple of days ago. I had been sweating you out somewhere about there when the fighting broke out and I had rather written you off!

Hope the letter via Lubbock caught up with you. I enclose a page of it which stayed here. We had a fire – not serious – but my correspondence was messed up and I either wrote another page or the one enclosed or just didn't enclose the original – can't remember which.

For God's sake be careful in the Sudan – I've only just heard of two young Americans murdered in their car a couple of months ago – en route down here. A very *light* and non-antagonistic protection is a couple of "Aerosol Bombs," typical fire extinguishers which temporarily blind anyone who is rude.

You'll be alright here, I hope, but Africa is really boiling up. The refugees from the Cameroons are pouring in. New Guinea – to jump a few miles – is on fire with head-hunters from the hills in war paint, with spears, bows and arrows and slings ravishing Rabaul, the capital. The whole world seems to have gone mad.

If you get into *serious* difficulty after Egypt – wire me!

Major S. Small, *R.C.A.*
    c/o Lieut. Col. Julian Pagett,
        2nd Battalion
            Coldstream Guards
                Gilgil
                    Kenya

I *might* be able to help as I do the odd piece of work for the Limeys, and might bulldog my way up to you. You can also *burn* this up when you've finished.

The British Military Attaché at Khartoum will know you are coming. His name is Colonel Hilary Hook, British Military Attaché, B. Consulate, Khartoum. Don't know him well, but he's a friend of friends who have fired off an epistle.

You are getting quite well known by now as I'm passing the word along to anyone you might bump into. I'm most serious about you having a house here for as long as you want it and come and go as you please. Hope you did get my lengthy "Lubbock" letter as it was full of plots and plans.

Life goes on fairly quietly. Kenyatta is out this month. New elections are on the horizon. The really grubby oathing is starting again. People rabbiting daily. (*Rabbiting* is a really "dirty word" out here now.) Races, polo, dances, military reviews, etc. The flag is flying and old Kenya is going down like the *Titanic*.

There are quite a lot of American tourists out here. A Princeton '20, his wife and a "lady friend" arrived today to say hello. Friends of friends of friends. Roy Ryan came out to lunch on Monday. He owns the Mount Kenya Safari Club. The Bermuda Dunes Club in California, a plane (club) in Bermuda, financier, Switzerland, and Monte Carlo, etc. Struck it rich in Texas and has kept piling it on. Originally from Minnesota he's a real character for Sinclair Lewis. The most unkind thing he did was to bring his 17-year-old daughter and a friend of hers along. After lunch we went bird shooting and got caught in a thunderstorm. I'm no prude, but it was pretty darn evidential that the only thing the fillies had on were Brooks Brothers tennis shirts, and it was crucifixion in this womanless country.

To add fuel to the fire – he sent out two lithe, lean, tanned Vassar graduates the next day, and the only thing worse than no woman is *two* women on an isolated African farm.

Kenyatta is about to come out of "restriction" and we seem due for more elections around November – probably when you arrive. Kuwait seems settled for the moment. I hope to ship over to Trucial in Arabia to spend a week with a friend in the "Scouts" on patrol in the desert, and come home via Aden and Bahrain where some regiments are garrisoned and I have a lot of old pals.

Have a couple of Salukis waiting in Trucial and hope to pick up a hunting falcon or eagle. Can't think of anything more of interest. Will send on the R.A.S.K. data on roads out of Cairo as soon as they arrive. *Please* let me know if there is anything at all I can do. It is raining now so all ranch work has ground to a halt.

I've just talked to two majors in the Coldstream who've blown in with their wives for some leave, and they said it would probably be wise to avoid wiring to me as a major via the military from Egypt as they'd role you as military spies, etc., so just use your own judgment – probably best just Sam S., Impala, etc. Hadn't thought of that one!

Well – all the best luck. They say God takes care of fools, etc. Looking forward to seeing you before long.

Cheers,

Sam

*   *   *

CAIRO, AUGUST 9, MORLAND HOUSE*

From Alex we took the new highway, sleek and glossy, and the citizens liked to sleep on it. Their animals wandered all over it, chewed their cuds and napped on it. The truckers drive right down the middle on top of the white dividing line, thus leaving two half-lanes on either side. Seductively fast. Weaving among man and beast, we thought we had left the animal and human clutter behind and hit 60 when the machine began to swerve and fishtail all over the road. I didn't know what was happening until we managed to pull over, get off, and examine the damage. A punctured rear tire. Had it been the front, with two riders and heavy luggage, we might have flipped. The front tire stands the nail up to jab into the rear tire, is what they say.

We got out the toolkit and went to work. We removed the tire and pried the inner tube out. By running our hands around the inside of the tire we found the culprit, a brand-new shiny nail, which we yanked out with pliers; then we patched the tube and blew it up. Joe dunked it in a nearby canal to see if bubbles came out. It was a hot and sweaty hour's work in 100° heat and 100 percent humidity with these crazy Egyptian truckers screaming by, hanging out the window and yelling God-knows-what obscenities.

First impression of Cairo: everybody in pyjamas with the drowsy languid look of people who have just got out of bed.

AUGUST 10, CAIRO

Cairo is *big* (the fifth largest city in the world) and surprisingly modern and Western. We were busy with visas and other time-consuming trivia. First stop: the Egyptian Museum, which is huge and would take many visits to see all. All the gold from the tomb of King Tut is there (*rooms* of it), plus thousands of other relics. The mummies surprisingly unimpressive: we dug up better ones in Peru; and they didn't compare with those at the Museo Nacional in Lima.

From Herodotus, *The Histories*:

> When the wife of an eminent man dies, or any woman who was particularly beautiful or famous, the body is not handed over to the embalmer straightaway. They wait three or four days before doing so. The reason for this is to stop the embalmers from having sex with the woman.

We are staying in a comfortable boarding house near the Nile between the U.S. embassy and the Hilton. We got our visas for the Sudan. We planned to travel by boat and train as the roads were flooded in the rainy season. The ticket for the 1,400-mile trip cost $15 (third-class deck passage).

We are continually besieged by students and teachers who beg us to answer questions and air our views. It is not easy to answer questions like these:

"Why does the U.S. support Israel when she drives the Arabs out of their rightful land and wages war against Arab nations?"

"Why does the white man hate the black man in America? Are not all men equal?"

"Why cannot the U.S. send a man into space like the Russians?"

"Why does President Kennedy hate Dr. Castro? Did not Castro free Cuba from the villain Batista?"

"Why does the U.S. attack a small country like Cuba?"

"Why does the U.S. have as allies France, Britain, and Israel, when they attack the Egyptians at Suez in 1956, slaughter the Algerians in Algeria, and the defenseless Tunisians at Bizerte?"

"Please explain Berlin."

AUGUST 11

Up at 4 a.m. to climb the Great Pyramid at Giza.

I'm worried about Joe: he hasn't been the same since Zuwarah. Not so much the wound, but the shock – that bullet seems to have knocked the stuffing out of him. For the tenth time I swore not to tell. I don't quite know why, but he doesn't want to let it out. Maybe Confederate pride. Doesn't want it known that he got shot in the back.

We have been warned that it was forbidden to visit the Pyramids without a guide. And absolutely forbidden to climb, in order to preserve the integrity of these colossal, timeless monuments.

From the guide book:

The Egyptian Pyramids, usually of stone, are square in plan. Their triangular sides, directly facing the points of the compass, slope at an angle of about 50° and meet at an apex. Each monarch built his own pyramid, in which his mummified body might be preserved for eternity from human view and sacrilege, and into whose construction went years of time and measureless amounts of material and labor. The three Pyramids at Giza, all of the IV dynasty, are the largest and finest of their kind. The Great Pyramid of Khufu or Cheops is one of the Seven Wonders of the World and the largest pyramid ever built. A solid mass of limestone blocks covering 13 acres, it was originally 756' along each side of its base and 482' high.

According to Herodotus, Cheops bankrupted his country and even prostituted his own daughter to help pay for the Pyramid (which must have made the poor girl the highest-priced whore in history).

How it was built remains a mystery. The ramp theory has been discredited because it would have to have been as high as the Pyramid itself and miles long. Herodotus wrote that the Egyptians worked in gangs of 100,000 men for three months at a time (the duration of the inundation); that the Pyramid was built up like a flight of stairs using wooden levers; that they finished off the topmost parts of the Pyramid first then the ones just under it, and ended with the ground level and the lowest ones.

Herodotus' description needs some deciphering.

Over the Nile bridge on the machine and out into the desert. At this hour the air is clean, cool, fresh. You want to ride on forever. The sun was just flaming the eastern horizon when I got off the bike. Not a soul around at this hour. The drago-men, guards, hawkers, and beggars all still asleep. But where? Not a shack or tent in sight. My main concern was that the machine might be stolen or confiscated while I was up. Must hide the bike. I pushed her behind a pile of rocks and locked the steering mechanism. Hoping for the best, I looked for a way up. But how? These limestone blocks were 6' high, some bigger. No way to climb over. Finally, I spied a narrow trail winding among them, one probably taken by millions of sightseers – pilgrims, slaves, soldiers, Hittites, Persians, Alexander the Great, Ptolemy, Howard Carter, Disraeli, Mark Anthony, Gen. Kitchener, Churchill, Herodotus, Copts, Israelites, Phoenicians, Greeks, Romans, Cleopatra (maybe not), Caesar, Nubians, Napoleon, Flaubert, T.E. Lawrence, Durrell, Rupert Brooke, Percy, et al. for the last 5,000 years or so. Now me.

So up I went, like a mountain goat, leaping from stone to stone, always keeping a vigilant eye on the machine as she became smaller and smaller. I was prepared to plunge back down the instant I spotted anyone tampering or attempting to steal. I should have encouraged Joe to come with me to keep watch while I made the climb. We guard her with our lives: she is our lifeline to this grand adventure.

The higher I climbed the wider the desert became. I could see all of Cairo, wreathed in the smoky haze of early-morning cook-fires; and the Nile, snaking away north and south with its green fringe of palms and numberless irrigated plots.

Here was the cradle of civilization; and a delicate, vulnerable cradle it is, suspended, as it were, from an umbilical of green, threaded between beauty and nothingness, nothingness and beauty. Which is what the desert is. That monument is part of the desert. These gigantic stones were cut and shaped somewhere in the desert, and transported on that fragile ribbon of green.

The Great Pyramid took 20 years to build and consists of 2,300,000 stone blocks, average weight 2½ tons. The construction was effected not by slaves but by free peasants, and the entire nation was organized to do it. The stones were moved during the inundation, which occurred each year with strict regularity, depositing a layer of rich sediment on the fields. Cultivation ceased, making transport over flooded land relatively easy.

Herodotus:

When the Nile covers the land, only the towns are visible above the water, and they look like nothing so much as the Aegean Islands. The rest of Egypt becomes an open sea, with only the towns rising up out of it. So under these conditions people take ferries not just across the river, but right across the plain!

A canal was built to Giza to bring stones to the foot of the Great Pyramid.

If the above figures are accurate, and my long division serves me correctly, the massive blocks were laid at the rate of 315 per day! Nearly 800 tons! And that's working 365 days of the year! Not including the polished limestone casing.

There is something fishy about these figures. They don't add up. That number of huge stone blocks could not possibly have been quarried, transported, hoisted up, and laid in the specified time period. (The lifetime of the Pharaoh.) Could it be that the Great Pyramid at Giza is not made of solid stone?

Anyhow, the canny Egyptians managed it, and we think of them in their pyjamas, smoking hubble-bubbles, their women veiled or locked away. Only a god could have mobilized the population. I guess that's what Cheops was – a god.

One advantage about climbing a perfect geometrically engineered pyramid compared, say, to a mountain or a volcano, is that, no matter how high you climb, you can see all the way to the bottom. The machine, now about the size and configuration of an albino ant, remained undetected and unmolested behind the boulders. The Egyptians were still snoring in their pyjamas.

I was glad I had made an early start. It took about an hour to reach the summit or, more accurately, the apex of four perfectly formed triangles leaning together, whose shadow, now projected by the rising sun, pointed like a steeple straight toward New York City.

It was good to stop and rest. It was cool up there. I was sweating and sat down for a few minutes, surrounded, not surprisingly, by thousands of names, initials, and scratchings of those pilgrims who had preceded me over the last few thousand years. Almost all French soldiers. When Bonaparte landed in 1798, he brought with him not only his army and his navy, but hundreds of scholars eager to explore the mysteries of ancient Egypt. And there I was, sitting on top of *the big mystery*. Beautiful work, hammer and chisel, most probably supplied by the guys in pyjamas who guided soldiers up to the top. A cool breeze flowed around my shoulders as I scratched my initials into the stone with the awl of my Swiss knife – pitiful, minute incisions to be scoured away by the next sandstorm. Then I bounded down, anxious about the security of the machine. Still not a soul stirring, not even a camel.

When I got back to the hotel, Joe had just woken up. He was looking stronger, not so pale, and was sipping from a glass of orange juice. I felt as though I had been to the moon, or as close as you could get to it without your feet leaving the ground.

*

To give an idea how old the pyramids are: Cleopatra (68–30 BC) lived closer to the time of the construction of the Empire State Building in New York (AD 1930) than to that of the Great Pyramid at Giza (2,680 BC).

We went to El-Muski, a section of Cairo devoted to the market and the bazaar: a huge labyrinth of a thousand tiny streets and shops where the scent of jasmine, mingling with a hundred spices, intoxicates. There were exhibitions of strongmen, fire-eaters, and ascetics on their beds of nails. Most fascinating, though, were the thousand different faces of a thousand different origins – especially the faces of women. Cairo is more liberal than the desert; the women bolder.

Joe may have been down and out, but his alcoholic energy is remorseless. Each drink is like pouring more gasoline into an engine already going flat out. At the Bar Safari he picked up a heavy stone ashtray and started banging it on the table. The drinkers loved it, but the owner came over and accused him of damaging his property, and threatened to call the police. By the end of a very long evening I felt, morally and mentally, I'd been beaten black and blue with a tire iron. All in the name of devotion: with Joe, learning does not come without pain.

AUGUST 15, STILL IN CAIRO

I finished reading, for the second time – the first time having been at Princeton, when I wrote an essay for Prof. Halpern on the Czech arms deal – Gamal Abdel Nasser's *Philosophy of the Revolution*. Obviously, the man is no intellectual; I failed to detect even the seeds of profound revolutionary thought.

The calls to the American and Russian revolutions were far more eloquent. First and foremost he is a military man only vaguely aware of the role which must be played by Egypt in the Muslim world. His hatred of Jews carries an intoxicating appeal among his fellow Muslims. Runaway Nazis have found a safe haven in Egypt.

However, in his rather naïve revolutionary philosophy can perhaps be found the fundamental but crudely stated principles alluded to by Camus in *The Rebel*, i.e. stated originally by him or by other philosophers. Nasser emphasizes the need for reform and the unrelenting fight against imperialistic forces within Egypt. If Camus stated that the most important element in any revolution is that it must not stray from its original precepts, then Mr. Nasser proves his sincerity by following through with his early revolutionary ideals. And it is this sincerity and belief that has got the people of the U.A.R. on his side and taken them along economically, politically, and socially since July 23, 1952.

No astute thinker, Nasser, but he turned out to be an effective politician. Even as dictator, he is sincerely promoting the progress and development of the U.A.R. and its citizens.

We picked up a pile of mail at American Express. My mother persists in sending me wedding invitations and even my N.J. driving license in the hope of luring me back home. Citing the perils of Kenya, she begged me to telephone, but that would have meant waiting in a long line at the P.O. She has to be content with the long letters I send from each major stop, detailing our adventures so far.

We are planning to leave Cairo for Aswan, where we will catch the steamer-train for Khartoum. We hope to spend two more weeks in Egypt in order to visit the early-dynasty ruins in Upper Egypt, some of which will be inundated when the High Dam is complete. We have tickets to take the steamer from Aswan Sept. 2, which should put us in Khartoum Sept. 6 or thereabouts. That is the plan.

Joe is still feeling low and so, after that long, grueling, hot, incredibly hot, trek across Libya, we are taking it easy in Cairo. We have visited the major museums, the great mosque, the Jewish and Coptic quarters, the markets. The *White Nile* is proving to be ideal transport for exploring the crowded streets and narrow alleys. Evenings are best: we sit up late in one of the innumerable cafés, sipping beer or their fabulous fruit-juice concoctions, nibbling lamb kebabs, drinking the strong, gritty, cardamom-flavored coffee, and jabbering with the curious, always with an eye on the machine.

How the Egyptians serve up lamb kebabs: Mohammed lifts six sizzling skewers off the charcoal embers and, gripping the round flat loaf like a pot holder, draws the skewers through it, releasing the meaty nuggets to nestle within the bread, on which he sprinkles ground cumin and salt, and hands it to you with a big smile and dainty paper napkin. And you are in heaven.

When you like their food, they like you.

AUGUST 18

The Nile valley, cradle of civilization, has become such a melting pot from multiple racial invasions from so many different directions that few indigenous characteristics can be discerned. One thing is clear: the black people are the descendants of slaves, or still are slaves.

According to Alan Moorehead, the great slavers were not the Portuguese, not the English, not the Americans, but the Arabs. They sailed their dhows down the E. coast of Africa from the Persian Gulf to Zanzibar, their HQ for forays into the interior of the dark continent. Whole regions of Uganda and South Sudan were virtually depopulated by their ruthless activities. When the wind changed, they sailed before the monsoon back to the Gulf, discharging their shameful cargo, destined for the households and harems of Kuwait, Baghdad, Damascus, Riyadh. Under pressure from reformers like Wilberforce, the West renounced this hideous trade. The Arabs never have.

One big difference: in Islam, when a slave woman or girl conceives a child by her Arab master, that child is deemed to be the legitimate offspring of the master, and as such is accepted into his household.

In Cairo the Muslim, Jewish, and Coptic districts are all mixed up, and in modern (in Egypt "modern" means the last 1,000 years) Cairo, Turkish, Greek, and Western European influences make for a manic, sometimes hilarious hodgepodge of cultures. Everyone is friendly, and the *White Nile* attracts crowds like a rocket ship from outer space. If we give one little kid a ride, a dozen others want to hop on board.

My view: atheistic communism will never make serious inroads in Islam. Muslims love their religion; they obey it. It is imbedded in every aspect of daily existence. It bestows value and dignity on millions of impoverished lives. They don't like to see their god pushed down a hole.

*

Out of this cultural confusion arises a profound allegiance to Nasser, a national pride, and, ominously, an intense hatred of Jews. If the political direction of the U.A.R. seems uncertain, it derives probably from the mass of variously assorted people bound together for the first time in history into a sort of nationalism, but confused in their aim except for faith in their man Nasser. More uncertainty derives from the struggle to throw off old Islamic ties which do not address twentieth-century problems, such as land reform, industrialization, etc., and in the often hesitant acceptance of Egypt as a nation, not just a melting pot of people and cultures.

AUGUST 22, HOTEL DE FAMILLE,* LUXOR

We came here by train, sitting up all night in the heat and dust, with the *While Nile* strapped to the seat behind. The RR guards will accept, for a tip, our magnificent machine, for which I pay a team of urchins a few pennies to clean and polish. She's easy to roll on and off a passenger car or stow in the baggage compartment.

It was a tedious trip from Cairo. We arrived exhausted, and me down with one of the fevers which have been pestering us for the last two weeks. Luxor, the massive antiquities notwithstanding, is a little European town reminding me of places in Peru. However, as I have spent the last two days in bed, I have seen little of it so far.

AUGUST 23

Luxor. A town of many shades, as seen through the haze of fever and fatigue.

Bats as big as ducks.

Spanish-style balconies reminiscent of Yurimaguas, upper Amazon, Peru.

A town predominantly Coptic (70 percent). I am told their language is the closest modern approximation of what the Pharaohs spoke.

Some questions have to be answered even in the face of confusing facts and circumstances. As we walked among the massive imposing columns of Karnak we asked ourselves: where exactly are we going? We are headed for the green heart of Africa. Assuming we get there, then what?

We summed up our options:

1. Use Sam's farm as a base, as he repeatedly suggested in his letters, to explore E. Africa: Kenya, Uganda, Tanganyika.
2. Head south, visit the Rhodesias, Mozambique, and South Africa, although this last, following the Sharpeville massacre, now seems the least desirable option.
3. Or go to Mombasa, to find working passage on a freighter bound for the Orient, as we did in Callao, Peru, one year ago.

The Winter Palace. We rolled up for a cocktail, but found the place locked down, closed for the season. The heat like a pillar in the middle of the room that we must circumvent each day. We were the only tourists in town.

The Colossi of Memnon. Faceless in Luxor. This happened all the time in Egypt. Succeeding dynasties knocked the faces of their predecessors' statues to emasculate their power.

I met a traveler from an antique land
Who said: Two vast and trunkless legs of stone
Stand in the desert... Near them, on the sand,
Half sunk, a shattered visage lies, whose frown,
And wrinkled lip, and sneer of cold command,
Tell that its sculptor well those passions read
Which yet survive, stamped on these lifeless things,
The hand that mocked them, and the heart that fed:
And on the pedestal these words appear:
"My name is Ozymandias, king of kings:
Look on my works, ye Mighty, and despair!"
Nothing beside remains. Round the decay
Of that colossal wreck, boundless and bare
The lone and level sands stretch far away.

Shelley's ghost has followed me all the way from Lerici to Luxor.

Luxor: the outer edge of ancient Egypt, reminding me of remote towns in the Peruvian rainforest, where Spanish fingers barely dipped.

An entire civilization, perhaps the most important in recorded human history, hanging by a sliver of river, a shiny green thread, the life-giver. What if the erratic creaking of the dark continent had split Africa E–W instead of N–S? Instead of meandering to the Med, the waters of Lake Victoria would have emptied directly into the Indian Ocean, maybe somewhere near Mombasa. Doesn't matter where. Egypt would have remained sterile and unproductive, like Libya. Madagascar would have become Africa's Manhattan Island.

*

Now we are *both* down with fever. Nevertheless, despite grinding heat and debilitating sweats, we hired donkeys to visit the Valley of the Kings, including the tomb of the mysterious King Tut.

Hemmed in by desert, Egyptian civilization, nourished through an umbilical of green, expressed its mighty energy in stone. The desert = death; it also encodes divine life. OK, some of us are atheists or, like me, not exactly agnostic but pseudo-atheist. Walk out into the desert at dusk, by yourself, as far as you dare. Hold your breath, and you will hear nothing, absolutely nothing, save for the beating of your heart. There is no soughing of wind in the trees, no murmur from civilization, no animal squeak or human voice. Stars like flares spill across the heavens in an avalanche so dense and close you want to reach up and stir them with your fingers. You are alone with the universe.

It was no coincidence that the three great monotheistic religions – Judaism, Christianity, and Islam – were all raised under the same thorny bush within a few desert miles of each other.

AUGUST 25

Aswan: swarming with Russians because of the dam.

Average temp in August: (over 24 hours) (*only!*)	107.5°F
Hours of sun (daily)	12
Rainfall	0
Days of rainfall	0
Distance from Luxor	215 km

Joe's mysterious fever drags on. He is not up to strenuous travel. So, in Luxor, it was decided he would take the train, with most of the luggage. I would follow on the machine along a road marked on the map by a red line paralleling the Nile to the east. Our plan was to meet up in Aswan and catch, if possible, the boat leaving the next day from Aswan, up Lake Aswan to our next destination, Wadi Halfa, on the border between Egypt and the Sudan.

AUGUST 25

About 6 a.m. I put him and the bags (including, thought-lessly, the spare tire) on the train and stopped for coffee and a sugary doughnut. (Like in Brazil, the caffeine lift from strong, gritty, cardamom-flavored Egyptian coffee is electric.) In my rucksack I had two liter bottles of H_2O and a supply of lemons which, I had been told by our guide through the Valley of Kings, were an ancient remedy against thirst, better than water.

About five miles south of Luxor the bright-red line petered out. The tar ended and I was bouncing along a rugged dirt track where previous traffic, judging from the marks in the dust, consisted of camels, goats, and a few barefooted locals. On and on, dodging boulders and ditches where the track looked as though it had been washed away by floods. How could this happen in a land where there is no rain? Maybe thousands of years ago. Time stands still in Egypt. Yesterday is the same as BC. Not one sign of any other vehicle having passed this way. Only the *White Nile* could have done it. My map was a hoax: potentially a lethal one. This was total desert. I wasn't worried about getting lost: I had the river on my right, sometimes a few hundred yards away, sometimes a wobble of green a mile or so off. Remembering Sam's warning, I stayed away from the river. Much as I longed to swim, I didn't want to be swatted into the water by a Nile crocodile or expose myself to bilharzia. To my left was a long escarpment of cliffs and ridges, probably packed with tombs and treasure.

As my watch ticked toward noon, the temperature soared. I had never experienced such heat. Compared to this, my memories of Nefta and Tozeur seemed positively air-conditioned. I never imagined it could get this hot on planet earth! In that temperature you don't sweat, you just evaporate. I was poking along at about 20 mph max., avoiding rocks and gullies. I was worried about the machine, whose horizontally opposed cylinders required more than this super-heated airflow to maintain a smooth running temperature.

The first puncture came about noon. I wasn't sure I could handle this on my own. Propping the machine up, I got the back tire off and found the thorn, an evil-looking thing about an inch long. I pried it out with the pliers that come with the toolkit, patched the gash in the inner tube, and pumped it up. One advantage of a BMW: the power is supplied to the rear wheel by an enclosed drive shaft and not by a chain, as with the English and Italian bikes, which has to be readjusted for tension after each tire change.

Exhausted, I sat on a boulder, sucked a lemon, and wondered if I should go back. I reckoned I had about another 80 km, or 50 miles, to go. Ahead lay an endless wilderness of sand and rock, where I could still be at the end of the day. I had passed the decomposing carcass of a camel surrounded by animal tracks. Jackals? Hyenas? Not one palm or acacia in sight. Nothing. I wasn't frightened, but apprehensive about what might come next. All exposed flesh already roasted: the back of my neck, my bare legs below the lederhosen. Once more the helmet had become intolerably heavy and hot. The bandana was knotted about my head. I dared not soak it in the Nile, even when I could have walked to the bank. But our guide had been right: the lemons produced saliva and assuaged my thirst. I was eating them whole and saving the water for an emergency.

4 p.m.: another puncture. It took me a long time to find the thorn, but impossible to locate the hole in the inner tube. I had no choice but to resort to the river, at this point about a half-mile away. I had serious misgivings about abandoning the machine. I had not seen one single other living soul the whole length of this trip, but I had no doubt I was being watched. You always are in Africa: some kid behind a boulder following your every move. Ready to pounce and steal the minute you turn your back. Things have a way of vanishing into thin air. At least no one could drive my beauty away. The rear wheel was missing, the front wheel was locked, and I had the key in my pocket.

So, with my inner tube, my pump and my patch, I walked to the River Nile. Normally, I had noticed, where the banks are flat and low, they are irrigated and divided into small plots where date palms thrive and crops grow. In this place, however, the bank was steep and I was able to descend to the river's edge. I took off my boots, cooled my feet in the water, and had a long look at this flood that had nourished civilization for thousands of years. No shrubbery about where crocs might lurk. Like piranha in the Amazon, crocs don't like fast water. The river: about ¼–½ mile across, not a swift flow, but with an eddying reverse current along the bank (which Huck Finn would have called "the easy water") where feluccas can sail upstream without rowing. No one anywhere in sight. I could have stayed longer, but it was already past 4 p.m., and the heat was at its height. There were still many miles to go.

I pumped up the inner tube, submerged it in water, saw where the bubbles came out, dried and patched it. I was weary from ten hours on the road, if road it could be called. The bright red line on my map had reduced to an animal track maybe a yard wide. It took constant vigilance not to collide with a boulder or blunder into a ditch.

My dusty but still gleaming machine stood in perfect solitude in this arid land that had succored millions of souls, founders of the modern world. Repairing the bike, I suddenly felt very tired. I had had nothing to eat since that coffee and doughnut in Luxor. It was stupid not to have brought along more food. I'd eaten all the lemons. I'm not sure I could have survived without them. I still had some water.

About 6 p.m. I spied houses ahead. It was like landing on another planet, one where children played in the street, men lounged in cafés, and women were busy doing the laundry and gossiping over the back fence. I had just arrived from outer space where no other life forms existed. The river had guided me the whole way. The cliffs to the east had walled me in, but I was led by the river.

At the Grand Hotel, where we were supposed to meet, I was told my friend had gone to the hospital. There I found him, alone in a spotless ward, weak, weary, but otherwise OK. The German doctor pronounced sunstroke and promptly put me into the next bed. The nurse handed me a glass of orange juice, which I drank, and then I slept for 12 hours. Thanks to the lemons I was not totally dehydrated.

AUGUST 27

Aboard the good ship *Issa* (or Jesus – a minor prophet in the Muslim pantheon), an ancient stern-wheeler, recalling the days of Rudyard Kipling or Mark Twain, inching upstream against the current, now strong in flood season, passing the half-drowned temples of Philae. We left behind the High Aswan Dam, being built at Nasser's request by the Russians. Hailed as a miraculous feat of engineering, it is nevertheless a controversial structure as it interrupts the annual Nile flood, which for millennia carried sediment to enrich the Delta soil, the key to ancient Egypt's prosperity and power.

We made the mistake of thinking we could tough it out in third class, sleeping on the deck with our heads barely insulated from the humming steel. Us, several hundred very black Egyptians, Nubians, and Sudanese, and three very pale and sickly Germans who admired the machine.

We came to our senses and, for a few dollars more, moved to a screened-in cabin upstairs. This heat just wraps you up, but we have become used to it. When you wake up, it is already 90° (plus humidity), mid-afternoon 100°+. Evening a blissful air-conditioned 80°, and we sat out on deck sipping the vodka I had bought from a Russian in Aswan. Ice supplied by Cook for a tip. *Bakshish* is the word. It does not exactly mean "tip," but more like sharing, a donation. If you've got more money than the guy waiting on you, you give a little extra, to level things out. Socialism – Muslim style.

The shore of Lake Nasser was strangely barren and deserted. Totally dissimilar to the teeming Nile Valley below the cataracts, there was nobody around. They say that thousands of

Nubians were forcibly displaced to make way for the rising water. They were out in the desert somewhere – homeless, abandoned, starving.

AUGUST 28

One unforgettable experience: a 3 a.m. stop at Abu Simbel. (Colossal statues cut from solid rock on the side of a mountain.) Visited by torchlight and moon. Impossible to describe the eerie and unworldly effect of these monumental (50–60' high) figures staring down on us. They were being threatened by the steadily rising waters of Lake Nasser, and there was talk of a plan of lifting them to the top of the mountain. We were privileged to see them, as millions before us had, that is before Thomas Edison invented the light bulb, with our guide and a flaming torch. In the tunnel beneath, bas-reliefs, carvings, and hieroglyphs. The whole experience – mysterious, weird, timeless. Unforgettable.

* * *

THE SUDAN

AUGUST 29, WADI HALFA

One of those poor Germans is down with typhoid. He'd had it for three weeks and done nothing about it, probably out of fear of being refused passage, or even of being thrown to the crocodiles. Poor guy, he looked half dead, skeletal and yellow. Consequently, our steamer was quarantined for several hours while everybody was inoculated. We had had our shots and were therefore exempt, but had to wait while everyone else got his. Meanwhile the *Desert Express*, ancient engine huffing and puffing, was waiting impatiently for us to board.

This train crosses the Nubian Desert, one of the most desolate on earth. It can be traversed by jeep or truck, but only in convoys of no fewer than three vehicles. Impossible for a two-wheel motorcycle, of course. No road, only a track following the RR. We met again the same group of cheerful Brits we saw on the Tunis dock. Huge Land Rover with roof rack, sand ladders, jerrycans for fuel and H_2O, whip aerial, etc. For *two weeks* they had been holed up in this remote outpost waiting for vehicles to make up the legal convoy. No flatcars available on the train. We merrily pushed the *White Nile* on board, wedged her between two seats, waved goodbye to our British friends fried almost black by the desert sun, and set off on one of the most unbearable trips imaginable.

It's not easy to describe the discomfort of this *Desert Express* rail trip across Nubia. We were now traveling "first class," having discovered it only cost a few dollars more. We sat up the whole way on cushionless wooden benches, dead tired and unable to sleep. The fine dust, seeping in through every crevice, became a swirling, caustic mist. I could actually *see* what I was breathing. Asthmatic, I could feel African dust coating my American lungs.

Desperate for a breath of fresh air, in the middle of the night I got down at one of the innumerable middle-of-nowhere stops and walked forward to the engine. The engineer and fireman, their coal-black faces further blackened by the nature of their work, welcomed me aboard. How could teeth be so white? It's the black that makes them white. Never had I seen people so black. I swear they were more than black. They were blue–black, the color of their coal. Their radiant welcoming smiles made the dust seem like history. In Egypt, even dust is history.

In Africa, ivory smiles make the continent sing. We recoil at the violence, the cruelty, and the poverty, but how do their feeble struggles compare to WWI, II, and the Bomb? If God is alive anywhere on earth, He lives in the hearts of the African, the South American, and other people who live in so-called godforsaken places we smugly refer to as the "Third World." And, anyway, most African wars were predesigned in the chancelleries of Europe.

I spent the rest of the night with my companions thundering across the desert (thundering = 20 mph). The ancient engine (English, naturally, probably of the same generation that still lugs trainloads of Indians over the Andes), like a stubborn but powerful beast of burden, was kept going by beating it ferociously with huge wrenches, twisting knobs, and making fine adjustments. The engine would not run at a constant speed, but went faster and faster until the track began to swivel on the sand, and received a violent hammering to slow down. An antique alarm clock hung on a cord from the engineer's neck; a boulder in the desert or the occasional mud hut told him where he was.

I took my turn with the shovel, hurling coal into the blazing hatch. It was satisfying to help out, to be part of their scene. I think they understood my need. I could neither hear nor speak for the clamor of the machine. When I climbed down at dawn, grimy from grease and coal, and staggered back to my "first-class" compartment, I felt I'd been to heaven or hell, I didn't know which. Maybe both.

AUGUST 30, KHARTOUM

We finally arrived, covered with dust and practically speechless with fatigue after 30 sleepless hours on the wooden benches of the Desert Express.

The streets of Khartoum are quiet, there are trees, the houses have gardens in between, with the river smaller and more intimate than the one in Cairo. The tall, black, elegant Sudanese (men) seem to float, not walk, in their ivory-white gowns. We are in Africa now — poor, slow, and calm — a far cry from the hectic bazaars of Egypt.

We knocked on the door of Col. Hilary Hook, friend of Sam, the British military attaché. He seemed astonished when he saw the machine parked outside. When we told him we had put her on the train to cross the Nubian Desert, our trip became a little clearer in his mind.

He welcomed us in. A white-robed Sudanese, gliding silently on bare feet, brought whiskey, ice, and a seltzer bottle. All this at 9 a.m. In Africa the contrasts are terrific. In the end you ask yourself: which was the more memorable – the hardship, or the relief? The answer is neither. Or both. One defines the other. Together they make the adventure unforgettable.

Col. Hook, who seems to have spent most of his adult life living under canvas, jungle and desert, in Asia and Africa, all over, longs to return to that outdoor life. He complained about the hectic social life he is now obliged, as military attaché, to lead. Poor guy, he is now plunged into a ceaseless round of embassy cocktail parties; what he wants is to be back on the savannah with his gun.

Our experience is limited compared to his, and what we expect from the experience was sort of outside his ken. Just as his vast experience, in a world (the British Empire) which is disappearing, is way beyond ours.

We raised our glasses: to experience.

Mrs. Hook grew up in Nanyuki in Kenya. She and Col. Hook were married in Nanyuki. Col. Hook's brother lived there. They both know Sam and say he is a fine fellow, also that there is no security worry in Kenya. All is calm; there is no violence. Mau Mau days are over.

My mother will be glad to hear this. I keep begging her to *open* the invitations, answer them, and *tell* me about the weddings, etc., rather than just forward them to me.

SEPTEMBER 1

I have come down with yet another mysterious, low-grade fever, aggravated by oppressive heat. Joe has glandular swellings, and neither of us feels energetic. Nevertheless, a few hours after arriving in Khartoum we found ourselves shaking hands with Mr. Ibrahim Abboud, the Prime Minister, at a polo match. (Polo was one of Col. Hook's passions.) We also met the Moores, the U.S. Ambassador and his wife, plus other sundry dignitaries and officials, all of whom played polo together. Men only, that is; the women watched, as did we.

At Princeton, Joe was a member of the university Polo Club. He had a vivid memory of J. Robert Oppenheimer, father of the Manhattan Project, whose home he visited to raise money for the Club, mixing one of his famous dry Martinis. He also remembered woolly-headed Albert Einstein padding solo along campus paths.

The Institute for Advanced Study at Princeton, directed by Oppenheimer, provided a safe haven for leading scientists, writers, and intellectuals from all over the world: many, like Einstein, von Neumann, and Thomas Mann (*The Magic Mountain!*) were refugees from war-torn Europe. And George Kennan, ex-ambassador to Moscow, author of the so-called "Containment Policy" for the Soviet Union, whom we met on our return from Peru.

Oppenheimer contributed $50.

The Khartoum polo ground, like Bourbon Street in New Orleans, is where the black and the white folk meet. You get the feeling the two races wouldn't like to be cooped up together for long.

The Sudanese are the blackest people I had ever seen: blue–black, blacker than black, some with the shine of some exotic form of anthracite. Nearly all, including the P.M., bear tribal scars on their temples and cheeks, varying in size and length depending on the customs of their tribe. Some of the cuts are deep, and have splayed out into wide scars.

SUNDAY, SEPTEMBER 3, 1961, KHARTOUM

We both had complete physicals from the top doctor in town, a Greek, recommended by Col. Hook. He found no traces of malaria, bilharzia, or any other bug in our blood. So these fevers remained a mystery. "African fever," the doc called it: something you come down with in Africa, and which leaves you when you leave. And he was Khartoum's leading medic. Could be worms.

The *White Nile* is still running smoothly and has proved to be a practical form of transport in Africa. When the going gets tough we slip it onto a boat or train, no problem. Jeeps, cars, etc. are more difficult because in many parts of Africa (i.e. the Sudan) by law you have to travel with two or more other vehicles together, and sometimes have to wait weeks for another vehicle to come along. Often awkward to place a large vehicle on a train or boat. We bumped into our English friends again, who we first met on the Tunisian dock. At one point they were 2,000 miles ahead of us. We caught up with them in Wadi Halfa, where they were stranded for *two* weeks. Must have been absolute hell. Now they are in Khartoum. They have spent $300 in shipping costs. Us: $20. Actually there is a whole group of us traveling up the Nile – Danes, Germans, English. We have been successful thus far in making a good trip of it because: 1. we have no schedule; and 2. the machine gives us flexibility and freedom.

SEPTEMBER 4

My map of the Sudan shows a country as big as Europe. Travel in the Southern Region is restricted due to the primitiveness of the tribes, something the government is extremely sensitive about, so we have to get special passes. The south black and mainly Christian; the north 100 percent Muslim. Here is a country very interesting anthropologically. Some studies are being conducted on southern tribes whose ways have not changed in centuries. Meanwhile the never-ending contest between the black south and the (sort of) white north. Christianity vs. Islam. It is all about Muslim contempt for black African Christians, even though many Muslims are blacker than black themselves.

Col. Hook has found us accommodation at the University of Khartoum medical school.

He also directed us to Niko's, a pleasant outdoor riverside café, where the evening breeze off the water refreshed after the long torrid day.

Niko, a Greek, serves up chargrilled chicken, tough but tasty – which you dip into a fiery sauce – French fries and ice-cold Heineken – all for a couple of dollars. Niko liked our custom, because when we rolled up on the machine, a group of young people invariably gathered.

The *White Nile* announced our arrival. It identifies us in Khartoum. The citizens have not seen another machine like it. Those who could read expressed their approval of the moniker.

Niko took our orders while the tables near us filled with students from the university. They sipped Coke or juice while we wrapped our grateful mitts around his frosty brews. The undergrads were eager to practice their English and air their political views.

SEPTEMBER 5, UNIVERSITY OF KHARTOUM

The plight of the Student Union is probably characteristic of the role students play in Middle Eastern politics and probably in underdeveloped countries all over the world. There are peculiarities: the current military junta does not permit the existence of opposition parties. The penitentiaries of the south are filled with political prisoners from the north. The Student Union represents the educated elite of the new generation who will one day govern the Sudan. Although it is split into several factions, the Union is united in its opposition to the present regime. However, their rebellion is compromised by the fact that few of them know anything about their own country. The fact that they are completely ignorant, or intolerant of what they do not know, does not augur well for the future of the Sudan.

The Sudan is ten times bigger than Britain, but so far we have not met one student who has been outside the capital.

The Student Union represents a semblance of opposition but, since any form of opposition is against the law, the government does not recognize it. It regards the S.U. as a provocative and dangerous foe but cannot overlook it. It attempted to weaken the S.U. through non-recognition. (Cf. the U.S. position toward Red China.)

Since the positions taken by the S.U. are basically incompatible with those of the government, there was but one alternative: to go underground and operate without government approval, grooming the swelling popular support for the eventual overthrow of Abboud and his junta.

On the other hand, the government needs to cooperate with the students, as the future of the country lies with them, and ministers are anxious to preserve the university as a forum for free exchange of ideas and unrestricted discussion. Also, the students would like some understanding and/or contact with the government. But, through sheer provincial idleness, they are bereft of belief and ideas. Thus the only means left to the S.U. is to work for out-and-out revolution. We haven't seen much evidence of this among languid young men in their white skullcaps and ivory gowns, sipping tea and playing Parcheesi. But this is Africa. People have their own time frame. Like the river flowing softly but ceaselessly, things just eventually, slowly evolve.

Again, as I already noted, the students are completely ignorant of their own country. They don't like to talk about it. Few have ventured outside the capital. Each night they pedal home on their bicycles. We told them we were headed for Juba. Some had no clear idea where Juba was. (On the Ugandan border.) They didn't seem interested in anything that was not right there in Khartoum, an inauspicious sign for young people who one day will be the leaders of this huge, mysterious country.

Mr. Abboud seems to be doing a fair job. At the polo ground where we shook hands, he gave off charisma and charm. (All dictators have it—Hitler, Mussolini, even Franco.) Col. Hook said he directs all his attention to the country. Minor dictators like him are seldom heard in international forums, but he was recently in Belgrade. Hassan Beshira, whom we also met, a polite military man, was apparently the *éminence grise* behind the government. He struck me as dignified and unpretentious, characteristic of his gov't.

The gov't calls itself non-political and non-racial. Nothing could be further from the truth. The so-called "white" Muslims rule the north and have all the power. The "black" south is Christian, thanks or no thanks to the efforts of British missionaries. Nobody in Khartoum pays any attention to the blacks: they are considered inferior. All the signs are in place for a major human conflict.

SEPTEMBER 7, KOSTI

We took the overnight train down to Kosti. We now travel first class and had a comfortable compartment, but the rain came in through the roof and soaked us. (When rain falls, the train stops, due to shifting sand, or sand turning to mud under the tracks.) The rain fell for five hours and, with pure African logic, we arrived five hours late. In Kosti the boat was waiting for us.

At Khartoum the river divides. The Blue Nile pours down from the Ethiopian highlands where it rises, with the White Nile flowing due north from due south, through the Sudd, a vast water-logged swamp (as big as Britain), the nemesis of Victorian explorers, from its source which, as Speke verified, is Lake Victoria.

No education for women: you can't help but be offended. The kitchen, the bedroom, and the veil. Traditional male Islam is fundamentally blinkered in devaluing women. Half the population prevented from participating positively in education, law, medicine, business, and every other field where women excel and which would help their nations prosper.

As long as this tradition persists, Islam will remain stunted. A man with one leg. Who would have ever heard of these countries if they didn't have oil? And when the oil dries up, who will be left to pick up the pieces? The women.

We rolled the machine onto the good ship *Marra* and secured her with rope to an iron railing. I paid a kid to keep an eye on her before heading up to our cabin.

"Yas, mastah, I will sleep right here. I will guard this lovely day and night."

We have a two-week voyage ahead of us to Juba in southern Sudan. The price difference between first class and sleeping-on-the-deck class was minimal. We were given: a screened-in cabin, two beds plus head, mosquito netting to fend off bugs. An outdoor desk for writing!

The *Marra* is not one vessel but six. Two barges lashed by rope and cable to each side of the main vessel, piled high with wood for the boiler, plus three barges up front loaded with cargo, vehicles, and about 200 Sudanese in various states of admirable nudity. (Men only.) Never have I seen such fantastically sculpted physiques: no wonder their brothers in America are Olympic champions. Plus the English "blokes" and their mighty Land Rover. One of their group has been felled by spinal meningitis and was left behind in Khartoum in a haze of penicillin. Apparently the pain is terrible.

The great stern wheel plunged us upstream toward the swamp. A propeller, I was told, with so much weed in the water, would soon foul.

SEPTEMBER 8, 1961

On the White Nile at last. (This part of the Nile is known as *Bahr-el-Ablad*, or White Sea.)

The wash-wash-wash of the wheel all night. Now we knew Huckleberry Finn. And Tom Sawyer. And Jim.

A violent thunderstorm raked us with rain and hail; morning rather cool beneath a pewter sky. The land beyond barren banks as flat as a billiard table – a beige one – the horizon studded by acacia trees. Lateen-rigged fishing boats beat effortlessly upstream in the "easy water." The tall black occupants in flimsy gowns smile and wave; in south Sudan everybody smiles and waves.

We had brought books, booze, and writing paper to content the empty hours ahead.

Joe's devotion owns you, or he feels it does, and is a blessing you ought to be grateful for. He feels it his duty to flay you, to tell you what an inconsequential, spoiled, semi-literate bastard you are. These drunken harangues usually take place between 2 and 4 a.m., preferably in some low-life foreign bar (Lima, Rome, Cairo, Khartoum) where no one will listen in, understand, or care. He picks these hours to catch you at your weakest, most vulnerable moment. By the time he finishes, he has dragged you from the swamp or sewer – whichever morass he initially plunged you into – to the top of the mountain where you can breathe clear air and see forever – all the possibilities of your brilliant career.

This procedure sounds pitiless but is not. This is how Joe expresses his devotion. He puts you up on the cross, pounds spikes into your hands and feet, but in the end yanks you down, alive. Sore as hell, sore in every part of your being, but still alive, more alive than you have ever been before. Little by little he resurrects you.

You aren't such a bad guy after all: you have immense possibilities, maybe talent. Maybe. It is a kind of catharsis, in which he puts you through an ordeal of learning more about yourself than you ever wanted to know, or thought you needed to know, or thought there was to know, or didn't want to know. It is a step toward self-knowledge, a painful one. He makes you question everything.

SEPTEMBER 9, ON THE BOAT

The more you see of the world, and by that I mean this part of this world (e.g. Africa and South America), the more you are staggered by the sheer glory of it, stunned by its elemental beauty, and the more you realize how little of it you understand. Here reside the richest mysteries of mankind. This raw world should not be viewed as a challenge, to be tamed or conquered, but as something completely original.

THE FASHODA INCIDENT, 1898

Toward the end of the nineteenth century, Britain was seeking to establish a continuous strip of territory from Cape Town to Cairo. France desired to establish an overland route from the Red Sea to the Atlantic. To make good this claim the French dispatched (May '97) Major J.B. Marchand with a small force from Brazzaville. After crossing 2,000 miles of unexplored wilderness, Marchand reached Fashoda on the Nile in southern Sudan on July 10, 1898, where he awaited a Franco-Ethiopian expedition from the east. Meanwhile General Kitchener's Anglo-Egyptian force had subdued the Mahdists in northern Sudan. When he heard of the French activities, Kitchener led forces upriver to Fashoda and, despite Marchand's presence, claimed the town for Egypt. The French government resisted for a time but, fearing war, ordered its mission to withdraw in March 1899. France yielded its claim to the upper Nile region and accepted part of the Sahara as compensation.

Hadj pointed out to us the site of the French encampment on the riverbank – just a couple of shacks half-hidden in the bush. Marchand marched from the Congo to get here; Kitchener sailed his flotilla up the Nile to confront him. This was the absurd pinnacle of Victorian hysteria over the "Land Grab" for Africa: this scrap over swampy real estate nearly precipitated war between the Great Powers. Hard to imagine. Nobody wants it now.

SEPTEMBER 10, MALAKAL

Big weed in the water. We are approaching the Sudd, a swamp the size of Great Britain. Maybe bigger.

I can't fathom, don't want to, the evangelical zeal that fired these missionaries, compelling them to stay so long in this remote part of the world in the hope of converting these so-called primitives to the Christian faith. To educate them (OK), to cure them of disease (of course). This makes sense, but to make such efforts to create a few half-baked Christians seems a wasteful and perhaps destructive effort. They were only isolating them from a tribal culture going back thousands of years. And to put clothes on these naked maidens – you might as well throw an overcoat over a leopard.

We saw the noble Sheelu (my phonetic spelling) – a tribe considered by the government to be so primitive and barbaric (and therefore so embarrassing) that no photos were allowed.

A typical evening encampment: ten or so dugout canoes nose like spokes around a central above-water mound that has been piled up from the surrounding mud. On this mound a fire was burning. Over this fire an animal of some kind was being turned on a spit. Around this mound stood the Sheelu, knee-deep in the water, all completely – I mean 99.9 percent – naked. Tall, slim, muscular warriors, some with spear in hand, stood beside young maidens with pointy breasts sticking straight out, tiny G-string hiding the pubic area but nothing else. Penises hung long and limp between shiny hairless legs. Evidently the proximity of young naked female bodies did not turn these warriors on; or maybe the tribal code forbade sex before supper; or maybe the maiden at your elbow was your little sister. With bodies like that you'd think they'd be having sex all the time.

SEPTEMBER 11

Now we are on the part of the White Nile known as the *Bahr-el-Jebel*, or Mountain Sea. The *Bahr-el-Ghazal*, or Gazelle Sea, feeds in from the western desert, where the gazelles live.

One cannot imagine a place more dreary than the Sudd: nothing but a vast marsh extending as far as the eye or binoculars can see. A papyrus swamp as big as Great Britain.

Our Nile is not a river any more, but a channel no more than 50 yards across (often much less), where the water manages to keep moving although it is choked with thick, heavy, floating weed. In search of elusive deep water, the *Marra* is continually running aground, that is, bouncing off huge, floating vegetal islands. Thus we are all the time stopping, backing and filling, which makes the trip even slower and more tiresome. The tedious progress of the steamer and the monotony of scenery drives one mad with Amazonian ennui. It has become a chore to read, eat, wash, and exercise. You sweat all the time. All daily activities have ground to a slow, relentless crawl. Like this old tub, the days just inch along. My only revenge is this diary, where I record how awful it all is.

In South America I learned that the rainforest and the swamp are overrated environments. Maybe not for the scientist, but for your average Joe: monotonous, monochromatic, monolithic, monosyllabic, mono everything. And that's what I think Joe has: mono.

The Sudd is not fit for beast or man. Inhabited by birds (millions), crocs (too many to count), and insects (zillions), it is just a mass of dull, green, dense, wet vegetation. But there are stunning images: two naked maidens of exquisite posture standing in a flimsy dugout canoe. With consummate skill they flung out the circular weighted net and hauled in the teeming flashing fish. Their smiles radiate across yards of water. And the missionaries want to put clothes on these people.

The reeds (papyrus) grow to a height of 20–30'; often it is impossible to see over them, even from the top deck. This adds to the claustrophobia and the inertia. Occasionally one sees trees that somehow manage to stand upright in this sea of rotting vegetation. Mainly it is just one green-brown carpet of reed and weed. The sky shiny-dull, like the bottom of a tin plate. When the sun comes out, it is stifling. Humidity approximating that of N.Y.C. in high summer.

Imagine Samuel Baker's agony when it took him *three months* to hack his way through! Malaria (anopheles) mosquitoes sing around our ears. We have each been bitten about 100 times. If we don't get it now, we never will. Two Sudanese below deck have it. We are taking heavy doses of paludrine. Immune for life.

Respite comes at sunset. We dig out the gin (there is not, as far as I know, another drop of alcohol on board) and the Schweppes Indian tonic water, bribe Cook for ice, slice limes Peruvian-style with the ever-sharp Swiss army knife, and nurse our G. & T.'s while taking in the flaming sky. Drink loosens our tongues, which have been tied in a speechless torpor all the long hot day. And the tonic water contains quinine, an early remedy for malaria. A drink with a double blessing.

SEPTEMBER 12, THE MARRA

In the Sudd the birds walk on water. Jesus-birds, I call them. They are rails. Big-toed, splay-footed, they stride from lily pad to pad.

Menacingly swinging their tails, a pack of prehistoric killers follows the lazy pace of this old tub. They are waiting for a handout from Cook in the form of slops dumped over the side. When this happens, a ferocious turmoil erupts in the water as the dinosaur descendants battle for every scrap. Then an eerie silence while they digest. As they reach the edge of their territory, others fall in and take up the hunt. Anyone falling overboard wouldn't last for more than a second, as a croc would grab you, embroil you in a "death roll," and tow you off to the larder. Col. Hook told us of an incident when a drunken deck-sleeper, Irish, allowing his leg to flop over the side, disappeared without a sound. Sweet dreams. No point in looking. The croc is a stealthy and cunning hunter. And he comes back for seconds. You don't want to be a sleepwalker on this boat.

The captain. Beard tinted orange with henna. Everyone calls him Hadj because he's been to Mecca. We have the upper deck to ourselves, where we can have our drinks in private. Alcohol offends Islam.

The good ship *Marra* was named after a mountain in western Darfur, Jebel Marra, 10,000' high.

SEPTEMBER 13

We passed another steamer headed downstream. On board, a group of young white Kenyans on their way back to Britain. The brief snatch of conversation as the two boats edged past each other in the narrow channel has left an uneasy impression. It was an aggressive and not at all friendly "Yank!" this and "Yank!" that, which makes me wonder what we are getting ourselves into. Ever since WWII the U.S. has been solidly in favor of independence for all African colonies, British and French. It was the one issue F.D.R. and Churchill disagreed on. Independence for all of Africa had come, is coming, or will come. Naturally the white colonials feel threatened. Their lives and livelihoods are set to change. Their days in Africa are numbered. And they blame America. Hopefully staying with Sam will mollify the situation. Uncle Sam.

SEPTEMBER 14, THE MARRA

One godsend on this deadly, slow-moving trip is this diary. Days of nothingness. We sleep a lot. A kind of sweaty, toss-and-turn sleep. We read, do push-ups and sit-ups to keep from falling completely out of shape, but there are many voids. A family of hippos wallowing in the slime provides a few moments' wonder; then you are back on empty.

Keeping the diary lends to this daily dilemma a modicum of discipline. It gives some shape to this formless life we are leading. And so easy to do. You don't have to make anything up. You just record what was in your head, before your eyes, your memories, and what you reckoned to be, on a particular day, the meaning of your life.

You pick up the pen. "Hey, I'm alive!"

"A good traveling companion is hard to find." Who wrote that? I did. To be with Joe is truly an amazing learning experience. If he had not been here I would be apprehensive of the future. (More than I am already.) But if I do have the courage to face it (the future), which now appears a complete blank, it is because he acknowledges this, feels this himself, shares this. Neither of us knows where we are going. My friends back home are busy shaping their careers while we flounder through the great gray green greasy unknown. After Kenya, then what? We don't bother to ask, because we don't have the answers. But what I am gaining is experience, vast experience on two primitive continents in the space of one year. But I wouldn't be doing this on my own. To have a friend such as Joe forges a powerful compact. We press on together. We encourage each other. Two heads are better than one. This is a voyage dictated by whimsy, idealism, a thirst for adventure, and an abiding faith in the unknown. We talk until dawn and doze through much of the clammy day. This is a voyage of ultimate luxury, because we are *learning* things about the world and about ourselves every minute of the day. Boredom can be a great teacher. You don't know anything until you know the boredom of it.

P.S. This diary is telling me to write. Put it down. Preserve it. Go on writing. No matter what I write, or want to write, or how I write it, I want to give it form. Form will validate it. Whatever I leave on a page, unless a mystery breeze whisks my notebook overboard, a snack for the crocs, these words will be with me forever. That was what the Pharaohs aimed at. Forever. That was what they got, but it took a pyramid to do it. I can achieve it on a single page. Forever.

*   *   *

UGANDA

SEPTEMBER 15, JUBA

The good ship *Marra* gave a last gasp and slumped into Juba. We gleefully leaped off the barge into the awaiting arms of the customs officials. Why didn't we stick around for at least one day? We could have visited the Greek shop, but no... We loaded up the *White Nile* and set off for Nimule, on the Ugandan border, 123 miles along a road that we were to learn was of dirt and was bad. After days sequestered on the *Marra*, we wanted to get going!

So we thundered off across this beautiful country, rolling wooded hills that reminded me of Peru. We began to see game – baboons and this huge prehistoric-like bird that sat on the road. We spotted many of these, and their plumage was magnificent – red and black. It looked big enough to snatch us off the machine. We also noticed elephant tracks and elephant dung, but no elephants. Not yet. We are in Africa now. Green Africa. Yellow Africa we have left behind.

Just like Luxor, the tar gave out after a few miles. We picked our way along a deeply rutted and puddled track. It soon became obvious that at this speed we were never going to make it to Nimule before dark. We stopped and consulted the map. It was a blank. Nothing between Juba and Nimule but this road, if you could call it that. We had to make a decision: go back to Juba, spend the night in that Greek hotel, and make a fresh start in the morning?

On this trip there was no going back.

Darkness fell. The jungle closed in. We edged along between two walls of tall trees. The headlight illuminated more animal tracks. We felt vulnerable, and where were we going to spend the night?

A sliver of moon gave us hope, but soon it was swatted away by advancing cloud. We saw the lightning and heard the thunder coming from a long way off. The machine had already keeled over a half-dozen times. Her horizontally opposed cylinders kept our bare legs from being crushed or scorched by the twin, super-hot exhaust pipes.

The storm hit. It was like driving into a waterfall. Solid rain, slamming thunder bursts, and lightning strikes that looked a foot wide. We heard trees crashing in the forest; we didn't know what we were hearing. The situation was becoming dangerous. We had no rain gear, we were making minimal progress along the flooded track, and we had started out with only half a tank of gas.

(We had been told the gas was no good in Juba; better to buy it over the border in British Uganda.)

The machine keeled over for the umpteenth time, and the light conked out!

There we were in the middle of nowhere, pouring rain, total darkness except for lightning flashes, thunder crashing overhead, big jungle all around with God knows what animals lurking. The only comforting sound being the purr of the *White Nile*. She was still running normally, as though nothing was wrong. Like the *Titanic*. No choice but to push on!

And so we did, another mile or so, 4 mph, riding and pushing, lifting her out of the mud, guided only by lightning flashes that briefly lit the track ahead. Then one freak bolt that seemed a yard wide illuminated a hut by the side of the track!

We were right next to it; had we gone ten feet further we would have missed it altogether.

We pushed our girl inside, out of the rain. I dug into the rucksack, got the flashlight out, and had a look around. Nothing there. Just a dirt floor, round in shape and mainly dry, and one very dirty single mattress. Probably stuffed with fleas: we didn't go near it. We lay down on the ground, one on each side of the machine, key out and steering locked. That was one of the scariest nights of my life. We did sleep a little, we were so worn out, but every 15 minutes or so I snapped awake to poke the flashlight beam into corners of the shack to see if any other critters, a cobra or a leopard, had crept in out of the rain to share our nest. It was hot, we were wet, and we were cold. Another storm hit, as violent as the first. Lightning flickered incessantly. It was as bright as day outside.

Dawn finally came. The sky cleared. We were still wet, pretty miserable, but otherwise OK. Relieved to see the daylight. The whole experience seemed like one horrible nightmare. I got out the toolkit, took the light apart, and inserted the spare bulb. As usual she started on the first kick.

On to Nimule, a collection of huts and a large school. The schoolmaster offered breakfast: strong Ugandan coffee, boiled eggs, papaya, and cornbread. Nothing ever tasted so good. We were in coffee country. The terrors of the Sudanese jungle were left behind; ahead – wide open spaces, and big game.

We crossed the border into Uganda, gassed up and headed for Gulu. Here began a series of unpleasant experiences which were to color the next two days.

(I am writing all this at the RR Hotel in Masindi, in Uganda.)

SEPTEMBER 16, GULU

The road south toward Gulu was hard, rain-packed sand – ideal for the machine. We raced along until we hit the mud. It was the rainy season; the track to Gulu soon became a slimy sea. For hours we shoved, pulled and straddled the *White Nile* through the mire. At one point we were almost run over by a red-headed maniac in a Land Rover. He thundered past us, sliding all over the track and deliberately, I thought, steered his vehicle into a rut next to us, drowning us in a wave of brown water. I could hear him hee-hawing like a donkey as he drove away.

We were to see him later...

Dead tired, we finally made it to Gulu, where we were put up by Col. Rhoades, whose name had been given us by Col. De Roebeck in Khartoum. These contacts are proving vital when traveling in this part of the world. Col. Hook, who introduced us to Col. De Roebeck, seemed to know everybody.

Col. Rhoades, a bachelor, age 50+, was soft-spoken, mild-mannered, friendly, and hospitable. Lonely. As glad to see us as we were him. He gave us whiskey, a bath, and bed. He was the head of the Labor Dept. in Gulu – part of the fast-disappearing British Civil Service in Uganda.

He took us to dinner at the local hotel, where I recognized the red-headed driver of the Land Rover, sitting with his elephant-hunting friend and white hunter. He was not pleased by my comments about his driving. Like in an old Western movie, it was decided to settle things outside. The African monsoon was flooding down from the sky. We traded a few ineffectual blows in the parking lot before being pulled apart. We went back to Col. Rhoades' cozy cottage and spent the night in a clean bed.

Joe: "Apologize to Col. Rhoades!"

I did.

SEPTEMBER 17

The next morning we set off for Murchison Falls Game Park, one of the top destinations for our trip.

Another horribly rutted road. At first we didn't mind so much as we were more preoccupied with the fresh elephant, buffalo, and lion tracks all over. Tall grass – 6' tall, both sides of the road – hemmed us in. We couldn't see the animals, but we could *smell* them, and all the time were expecting one to show itself in some disagreeable manner. After eight miles we reached the official entrance to the reserve, where there was a clearing, a few shacks, and a large sign designating the rules, one of which was:

NO MOTORCYCLES ALLOWED IN

We had a long and, we thought, friendly discussion with the African park attendants, who kept pointing to the rules. The rules. We had to go back. There was no way we were going back; it had taken a two-hour struggle in the mud to get this far. While we were talking a herd of about 50 buffalo came grazing past, one or two sniffing at the machine.

These animals, considered to be one of the most dangerous and unpredictable of African big game, seemed as peaceful as ordinary cows, but twice the size with huge horns and a definitely undomesticated demeanor.

We made it clear to the wardens that we were proceeding at our own risk. After our chat, during which we were given coffee and cookies, we set off again, right through the middle of the herd. We were terrified that one of these monster beasts might charge, but they paid absolutely no attention. Maybe they thought the *White Nile* was a cow, an albino buffalo.

The track headed off into the tall savannah grass, and once more we were shut in. We couldn't see anything. The park rule is completely sensible: on a motorcycle you have no protection. Plus the track at that time of year is virtually impassable for a two-wheeled vehicle.

The going got worse, with the track often submerged by last night's violent storm. At times the mud was a foot deep. We could not ride, only slide, mainly push. The machine must have tipped over 50 times but never stopped running. It took us four hours to cover the 20 miles to the lodge at Paroa. The ordeal wore us out completely. We were concentrating so hard on saving our transport we paid little attention to the big game all around us. We spotted some elephants about 50 yards off. They ignored us, and we were completely preoccupied with pushing the machine along.

As I look back now at the danger we put ourselves in, I think we must have been out of our minds. It just shows how obsessed we were with saving our beauty. If one of those beasts had charged, there would have been nowhere to run, nowhere to hide. There wasn't a tree in sight, just the thick, impenetrable savannah.

Finally we arrived in paradise – the lodge at Paroa. The man at the desk reminded us that it was strictly forbidden to enter the park by motorcycle but, since we had come all this way on the machine, we could stay. The lodge commands a panoramic view over the Victoria Nile. The countryside spectacular – lush, with rolling hills. Cloud formations visible for hundreds of miles, rainy and stormy in some places, bright and sunny in others. We were given a tent under a thatch roof – primitive yet comfortable. We showered and washed our clothes by treading on them in the shower. We pushed the machine into the shower and scrubbed her with the same soap, brushes and towels we had used on ourselves. She emerged bright white and shiny, as though she had never flopped a hundred times in the African mud.

At night we can hear the bellowing of the hippos and crocs down by the river. Occasionally, at night, we were told, an elephant would wander into the camp to raid the garbage dump. Then there was one frustrated old bull that used to tip over cars, pull the covers off you in your tent, etc., just for the hell of it. He was shot because the customers were complaining.

But I am getting ahead of myself...

We ordered cocktails at the bar and had dinner. For about 90¢ you get an eight-course meal. The people here eat so much we can't believe it – breakfast, lunch, high tea – all huge portions and much too cheap.

The chief warden who had welcomed us at the desk appeared at our table. He was what you might call the white-hunter type: tall, solid, not bad looking, heavily sunburned, but now drunk. He said he had had reports that we had been arguing with his "boys" at the park entrance. (This was untrue – there had been no argument; it was agreed that we were proceeding at our own risk, and we had shaken hands all around when we left.) Nevertheless, the warden didn't see it that way. He ordered us to leave the park first thing in the morning. There was no point in arguing: he was the boss and he was very drunk.

This is a huge blow to our plans. The main attraction of the Murchison Falls Game Park is the boat trip upriver, to the Falls, where you see crocodiles, hippos, and all the other game in their thousands. But he was in an ugly mood. We went back to clean sheets and got a decent night's sleep.

SEPTEMBER 18

We woke up in comfort, but hung-over and depressed. We were going to miss the main attraction of the park, something we had been looking forward to for weeks. At breakfast the warden was in attendance, arms crossed, making sure we followed orders. There was no point in bringing it up.

While the other guests boarded the boat that was to take them to the Falls, we pushed the machine onto an ancient ferry that crossed the Victoria Nile. This other half of the park, we were told, was the home for some 14,000 elephant, among other beasts. We must have seen most of them that day, long lines trailing one after another, trunk to tail, as peaceful as Babar and his family.

The track leveled out. We tooled along at 30 mph on rain-hardened sand – supersonic after yesterday's struggle. The warden had warned us about getting "flattened." Apparently when angered or disturbed, an elephant will not skewer you with his tusks or trample you, but grab you with his trunk, deposit you at his feet, and kneel, crushing the life out of you. However, like our buffalo on the other side of the river, these great beasts seemed benignly indifferent.

But we did get into one fix.

Joe was driving. Cresting a low hill, we spotted a lone bull elephant standing on the track ahead of us. We stopped, got off the machine, got out the binoculars, watched, and waited. We were in a vast green undulating plain without a tree in sight or a ditch to hide in.

Babar started moving in. We turned the machine around and retreated, only to spot a second elephant on the track behind. We stopped again, trapped by these massive beasts. We were about to be squeezed by two Babar bookends. Then, in no uncertain terms, the second elephant, ears flapping (a sign, we had been told, of irritation or aggression), started walking toward us. We turned the machine around again. To our relief, the first Babar had moved a few yards off the track and was yanking weeds out of the ground.

I was riding pillion. I whispered to Joe, "This may be our only chance. Go for it." (Memories of Libya.) He kicked the machine to life, and we cruised, slowly, 5 mph (we thought, friendly-like) toward the mountain. Then suddenly, inexplicably, our beauty shut down. We were no more than five yards from the wall of muddy gray. I could have gotten off the machine, walked a few steps, and patted his tummy.

Immediately, I saw what the problem was. BMW motorcycles have a plunge key, and Joe had not pushed the thing down far enough to make contact. The machine had somehow fired because the cylinders were red hot, but as soon as we started moving they cooled and the engine cut out. And there we were, eyeballing this beast.

I leaned over Joe's shoulder and hammered the key down with my fist. He kicked the machine back to life, and we darted away.

It was like an insight, or a blessing, or a warning. There we were, practically rubbing shoulders with these large, unpredictable, and dangerous beasts, and they had ignored us. I give full credit to the *White Nile*. For them she was some sort of sacred cow, and we were sitting on her. If we had been on foot, or had she been black, not white, the consequences might have been different.

After another mile we had to stop again for a female elephant and her baby. But there was no trouble. After about half an hour she moved on, encouraged by stones that a few blacks, working on the road, threw at her.

We made the rest of the 60-mile trek to Masindi without incident.

SEPTEMBER 20, AMBER HOTEL, KAMPALA

An extremely clean, neat, well-laid-out town. Fairly pretty, with floral parks, peaceful, dull.

The Ugandan countryside was magnificent all the way, with a lush green coloring those comfortable rolling hills. Ideal for European settlement, but in fact white people are not allowed to own land there. Everything is thoroughly integrated. It was, without doubt, a "black man's country." Still, the racial attitudes of some colonials are hard to swallow. You wince to hear their cruel, bigoted opinions. Their words shut you up. You don't know what to say or where to look. We are not talking about rednecks or hillbillies here, but pleasant, educated, middle-class people who know how to use a knife and fork. Uganda will soon be independent. Most of these people will go away. Maybe a good thing, too.

SEPTEMBER 22, TORORO

We rode along the shore of Lake Victoria to arrive at the Catholic mission, recommended by Col. Rhoades. In the afternoon, believe it or not, I got in a round of golf with Father Petrus, one of the White Fathers.

The mission golf course was groomed by goats. A small herd was pushed along the fairway by a boy with a stick.

Over dinner we got an earful of mission gossip from the fathers. It was the Catholics vs. the Protestants vs. the Muslims in the religious contest for Uganda. Sounded like the Muslims were winning.

A few nights ago we were sleeping in the mud, scared out of our wits. Now we were playing golf with White Fathers. That's Africa for you.

* * *

KENYA

SEPTEMBER 23/24, MOLO

We crossed the Kenya border and on to Molo, where we stayed with Col. Keighley and his wife on their beautiful farm. Friends of the Hooks in Khartoum. High here in Molo, about 8,000'. We crossed the equator at 9,600'. The country could be Canada, with pine trees foresting the great rolling hills. Chilly at night, and we sleep under blankets.

Every night a fire in Kenya, the most beautiful country I have seen. But so cold it is hard to believe we are still in Africa. We don't have warm clothes, having airmailed most of our luggage to Sam from Khartoum.

Kenya has been waiting for us ever since we planned this trip aboard the *Saturnia*. Now we are here. With all the misadventures of the past few days, I am hoping we won't be disappointed.

The Keighleys' place is a model farm of 300 acres. Well-tended lawns (one "boy" did nothing but push a lawnmower all day) and flower beds featuring the "red-hot poker" (aptly named). Three children – aged five, six, and nine. They are the cutest kids. We took them for rides on the machine. Also sheep, cows, pigs, horses, peacocks, geese, chickens, turkeys. Everything. A perfect farm in a perfect setting, where they lead a comfortable but well-earned life beneath a roof that might blow off at any minute. Crazy.

Theirs is typical of the situation many white settlers face in Kenya. For the past 12 years they have worked hard to create this beautiful nest. It is all they have. If, in the event of independence, they get thrown out of the country, they will have little money other than what they have sent to England to pay for their children's education. In the face of this uncertainty they seem very courageous, adopting a rather stoical attitude. In 1947 they were forced to leave India. Underneath, however, you grasp the apprehension: the possibility their whole world could be swept away.

SEPTEMBER 28, STANLEY HOTEL, NAIROBI

The knot in the pit of my stomach: got to fix the bike, locate the suitcase, help Joe to get well, and find a new direction.

OCTOBER 2, NAIROBI

The suitcase with all our clothes, which we had airmailed from Khartoum, has been lost by Scandinavian Airlines. Lost or stolen. Joe had literally all his possessions in the world in it. The notebooks with the poetry he had written on the trip. Our jackets, shoes, etc. So we have no clothes, except those on our backs, a few pairs of socks, underwear etc., which we carry in the rucksack.

We have spent five days vainly trying to locate the bag. Now we are sick of the whole goddamn business.

On top of this the machine broke down and is undergoing a series of complex repairs. The right-hand cylinder has burned out. Nairobi teems with competent Indian mechanics; they are entirely familiar with English bikes: Triumph, Norton, A.J.S., B.S.A., Royal Enfield, etc.; but they had never set eyes on a BMW with its horizontally opposed cylinders. So I cabled Munich requesting a myriad of miscellaneous parts: gaskets, cylinder heads, all kinds of bits and pieces that Ali, my mechanic, required in order to put the girl right.

Plus: Joe has been sick for the last two months with some sort of glandular fever. The doctors can't seem to do anything about it except say it will go away of its own accord. What he has is swollen and sore glands. Nothing too serious, I hope, but it makes him listless. He is definitely not his old self, not since Zuwarah.

OCTOBER 4, HOTEL QUEENS,* NAIROBI

Until spare parts arrive, the machine will take us no further, so we sat in the hotel lobby waiting for Sam's car to collect us.

Land Rover? Jeep? Pick-up?

A modest gray English Ford Sedan, complete with liveried driver, Hassan.

OCTOBER 5, IMPALA FARM,
NEAR MT. KENYA, NEARER NANYUKI,
KENYA COLONY, BRITISH EAST AFRICA

What else is there to say? We made it. About 5,000 miles across Africa, maybe more, + another 1,000 down Italy from Munich = 6,000 miles: that's the same as crossing the continental U.S.A. coast to coast and back again. We had some scary moments along the way, mainly due to lack of judgment on our part, which could have gotten us into serious difficulty, maybe even killed. But we were fortunate, and we owed everything to our utterly dependable BMW motorcycle, now deservedly resting and hopefully recuperating in Nairobi.

Sam was not at home. We had a look around. The first thing we noticed was the dogs.

Sam has 40 dogs! – every canine breed from Yorkshire terrier to Rhodesian ridgeback. And they are *everywhere* – curled up in the easy chairs, taking up most of the sofa, sprawled on the deck, in our beds. When you sit down, they sit down with you, and place large smelly hairy heads in your lap. When you take your shoes off, they lick your feet. In the middle of such a remote, wild, untamed wilderness, we are surprised to find ourselves surrounded by so many placid, friendly animals. Our own private, personal pet is a small, apparently harmless, yellow-and-white wire-haired mutt who goes by the name of Anthony Barkus. He attached himself to us the minute we arrived.

Plus, for reasons we do not yet understand, we have been assigned our own personal bodyguard: a Kikuyu named Massu. Dressed in skins, armed with a bow and quiver full of poisoned arrows, he warms himself over a charcoal brazier outside our door.

No Sam yet, only his "boys," and their women and children, all barefoot, slipping softly, with a tinkle of laughter, between their shambas and the main house. The kitchen is outside. Behind the house rises a high, rocky bluff where leopards lurk. Consequently, the dogs are locked up at night, because leopards favor dog meat. Even so, sometimes a leopard creeps in and drags one of Sam's pets away. (This from Hassan, on the drive up from Nairobi.) This does not erupt in a life-and-death battle between predator and prey, but is done in complete stealth. The leopard lies down beside the sleeping canine and throttles him with his jaws, basically closing down his windpipe and suffocating him without a whimper, and hauls him away from among his sleeping friends. Such is the leopard's strength and cunning.

Walking into Sam's house, unless you glanced out the window at the towering 17,000' high silhouette of Mt. Kenya, you might have thought that you were in fox-hunting Worthington Valley, Maryland. Fox-hunting prints crowd the walls; quantities of highly polished silver adorn the shiny surface of every table. The largest of these tables is in the dining room, long enough to seat a dozen, bedecked with silver candelabra centered around a large ceramic bowl, piled high with our mail.

Sam finally arrived. With everything else out of the top drawer, old school tie etc., his outfit did not surprise: a multi-pocketed Abercrombie & Fitch safari jacket, British military-style khaki shorts, cut just below the knee, knee socks and boots. Safari hat with brim turned up, Australian-style, on one side.

We were ready to embrace him, we were so glad to meet at last, but he fended us off with a wave of his arm.

"You know, boys." He glanced at the opened mail scattered over his table. "I've been here ten years, and in all those years, I haven't received as many letters as there are in that bowl."

With those words he established a kind of barrier between us. It is not easy to fathom the divide he meant to create:

resentment that we have received so much mail when evidently he has received so little? And the reason for that? Or because the letters come from a world to which he no longer belongs? Or that we are loved and missed and he apparently is not?

My mother had made inquiries about this gent who sent us the exotic invitation from halfway around the world. He came from a well-heeled family in Pennsylvania. He attended the Gilman School in Baltimore, which every year sent to Princeton a group of talented lacrosse players who, like half the ice-hockey team coming down from St. Paul's School in New Hampshire, naturally expected to be tapped for Ivy. But there was some sort of mystery: why had he left behind everything he knew and gone off to live alone in the wilds of Africa?

OCTOBER 6, IMPALA FARM

We went for a drive in the Land Rover (Hassan driving) to survey Sam's vast acreage. The house was built, he told us, before WWI by an aristocratic Austrian family. We visited the mini hydroelectric plant, dating from 1914 (when with the outbreak of WWI all Germans and Austrians were expelled from Kenya Colony), which still supplies the farm with 24-hour electricity. There is a pond, with a solitary male hippo in it. In season he bellows for a mate. It is hard to imagine a fat, wet mama hippo listening in, let alone waddling for miles across the thorny landscape to join this lonely Romeo.

Sam's land is plains, dotted with stiff thorn trees. The land dry and not very productive. He said he ran one cow per 20 acres. We didn't see a single cow. He said there was plenty of

THE WHITE NILE DIARIES

game around – lion, leopard, zebra, giraffe, elephant, buffalo, rhino, all kinds of buck, antelope, etc., and a solitary hippo! We saw ostriches and giraffe. The giraffe was a majestic beast of the rare reticulated variety, richly colored, which had found refuge on Sam's ranch. They canter so gracefully. Their hooves don't seem to touch the ground. We wanted to see more game. In Nairobi I had bought a telephoto lens and hoped to get some good shots. You really have to look for big game because this is not a reserve. Actually, the game situation is terrible. Fifty years ago herds of game wandered in their thousands over this area. Now you have to drive for hours to see a single beast. Numbers are dwindling fast and poachers don't help.

OCTOBER 7, IMPALA FARM

The Coldstream Guards are bivouacking on Sam's numberless acres. Three young officers turned up for a hot bath and supper. Sam possesses the only hot water tank for miles. We took turns bathing in the same water. The color was brown, not from our dirty bodies, but that is its color when it comes out of the tank. First one in got it plenty hot, the last one at room temp. But, first or last, the warm H_2O felt mighty good, after all the dust and dirt.

None of these young English officers, all about our age, have been to university, but to English "public" schools, like Eton College, before Sandhurst. They are impeccably behaved but, I thought, toward us, a bit condescending.

That Joe and I had just completed a trip by motorcycle from Munich to Kenya interested them, somewhat. Our adventures were all we were full of, and when our tales fell on deaf ears, we fell silent. We felt diminished by their lukewarm attention. It was strange: of all the hundreds of encounters along the way – Tunisian, Libyan, Egyptian, Sudanese, Ugandan, Kenyan – and the old Africa hands – Col. Hook, Col. Rhoades, Col. Keighley – the only ones who seemed indifferent were these young soldiers.

The conversation around Sam's table was about bird and big-game hunting, polo, racing – and especially the social scene in Nairobi. We were discomfited by the fact that these young officers, with whom we share the same language, religion and values, sort of ignored us.

Sam was in his element. He had served in the Canadian Navy during the war and, like so many of his ilk from the U.S. East Coast (my mother included) was an ardent, if not abject, Anglophile. All true style and refinements came from England, with primitive America still playing catch-up (my mother, a dyed-in-the-wool Republican, worshiped Churchill, loathed F.D.R.). I resented this brainless adulation, but in Sam's house kept my mouth shut. We were relieved when the young officers retired to their tents and their batmen. We went back to Massu and Anthony Barkus.

You have to respect these young English officers. They are, after all, highly trained professional soldiers of an historic, elite, and gallant regiment. But they are high-school grads as far as we are concerned. They have never focussed their attention on an intellectual subject, as college students are obliged to do. And they have brought with them their "public" school attitudes: "Wogs," "Pakis," etc. They haven't attended university because they have chosen the army for their careers, in a regiment famous for bravery in many battles over many years; but they sort of pulled rank on us and managed to make us feel inferior.

OCTOBER 8

More on last night:

There was talk about Jomo Kenyatta, who has recently been released from exile and returned to Kenya, and is now negotiating with the colonial authorities about a new and independent Kenya, which all know must some day come.

Kenyatta is no savage from the forest. He has studied in England, where he befriended Kwame Nkrumah, President of Ghana. Together they founded the Pan-African Federation. And what language do they have in common? Let's face it: England and English straddle the world.

For most of the white population of Kenya he is a blood-thirsty terrorist, and the possibility of him one day becoming the president of the country fills them with disbelief, fear, disgust.

I did not mention that at Princeton I had written a paper on the Mau Mau (for Prof. Halpern) and had learned about the atrocities committed by both sides — mainly by the Kikuyu against their own people, but also torture by the colonial authorities. Beginning with F.D.R.'s speech at the Casablanca Conference in 1943, America had been prodding our allies to relinquish their colonial empires. His words were not welcomed by his friend and confidant Churchill, who cherished his Empire and all the benefits that British law, language, industry, and culture had bestowed on the world. Hard to argue with that.

In deference to Sam, his pleasure of entertaining these young Englishmen, I kept my mouth shut. My knowledge of the Mau Mau would not have been welcome at his table. Everything I know comes from books. I haven't had to erect a chain-link fence around my house; I haven't lived in terror for the safety of my children; I haven't slept with a revolver under my pillow.

OCTOBER 9

Breakfast at Impala Farm is served on the veranda at five o'clock in the morning. For Joe and me the hour seems pointlessly early. After months on the road, arrivals and departures at all hours of the day and night, and many nights with no sleep at all, a couple of good lie-ins would have been absolute bliss. But no, if we want a decent breakfast it will be at 5 a.m. And more than decent it is: strong hot Kenyan coffee made from beans off a neighbor's farm, fresh orange and mango juice, oatmeal and/or fresh eggs from the farmyard, bacon. Enough to keep you going the whole day. At 5 a.m. the air is fresh and clear. You suck it down. You can see forever. Mt. Kenya like great lumps of vanilla ice cream. After breakfast Joe took a walk while I went back to the room and slept for another hour on a full stomach. Morning siestas are the best.

The house is built ranch-style, all on one level, from some exotic wood. A veranda runs the whole length of the house which faces down a long, widening, bowl-shaped valley. Rocky escarpments rise on each side, with the valley opening to a view of towering Mt. Kenya, 17,000' high, eternally snow-capped. The entire house seems to have been aligned to take in that majestic panorama. And, piled on the roof, a spreading purple bougainvillea.

The right-hand escarpment is home for a colony of baboons. Through the binoculars we watched the big males sitting lookout on the prominent rocks.

Of all our ancestors the baboon is the one I favor the least. They are ugly critters and very hungry. No animal charm whatsoever. The long snout and permanent scowl give them a brutal, predatory look. Like us, they are omnivores. They will eat anything — locusts, or your baby. Anything on the table. Massu told us leopards hunt them. I'm for the leopards.

OCTOBER 10

At 5 a.m. Sam is at his best, i.e. sober. We are beginning to realize that he is a paranoid alcoholic. There are bottles all over the house — hidden behind cushions, in vases, under chairs, etc., like Easter eggs. At dinner, always served in magnificent style by his loyal staff, he is generally incoherent.

Joe and I are growing increasingly edgy over having as our host out in the middle of nowhere a man who seems to be spiraling out of control. He is always friendly, but sometimes frightening. He rattles on, but often it is hard to follow the thread. We are totally cut off from the outside world. The Ford has conked out and the Land Rover is up on blocks. From day to day we wait for the mechanic to arrive from Nanyuki to get the motors up and rolling. So far no sign of him.

OCTOBER 11

Today at breakfast came an announcement that threw our visit into turmoil.

"Boys, last night I got word that a big contingent of Somali raiders is on its way here, headed in this direction. They're going to steal my cattle and burn this place down. We've got to fort up, collect guns, call in the neighbors, and defend ourselves. I hope you know how to shoot, because tonight you're going to be in the front line."

He finished his coffee, got up from the table, and walked away. Joe and I looked at each other: holy shit, what the hell is going on? Here we are, in one of the most beautiful, peaceful landscapes in the world, and tonight we are going to have to fight for our lives!

We thought but did not say: there's a crack British regiment camped a few miles from here. What have we got to worry about?

We didn't know what to do, so we did what we always did. We went back to our room and slept for another hour.

12 NOON

We didn't notice sandbags being filled. No Land Rovers arriving packed with guns and neighbors. Life was going on as normal. The usual murmur of chitchat from the kitchen. The gardeners digging away. Flower beds being watered. Dogs fed. House swept. Beds made. Ice bucket being filled. But no Sam.

And the sun gleaming off the eternal snows of Mt. Kenya. Anthony Barkus curled up between our beds.

A call to war, then silence. Our host was missing. We looked for him all over, but he'd vanished. We didn't know where to. With both cars out of action he couldn't have gone far. He wouldn't have wandered off into the bush. He wasn't that kind. He had been raised in comfort and was used to it. He owned one of the most beautiful homes in the world. Certainly one of the most romantic and adventurous.

The "crisis" had passed, but Joe and I felt unnerved by his announcement. We didn't feel wanted. We felt our invitation, preceded by so many letters and introductions, had already expired. We had worn out the welcome mat, even though we had barely set foot on it. It was like being at the wrong end of a magnet; after months of attraction, we now felt repelled.

"Where's Mr. Sam?" we asked Hassan – driver, barman, major-domo – as we headed toward the living room for the usual preprandial "gin and it" with our host.

Smile. Shrug. "Mr. Sam not feeling well."

It seemed like a conspiracy of silence. At least 20 Africans lived in their shambas behind the house. Gardeners, cooks, cleaners, various employees and their families. All friendly. Young women delicate and mysterious. We knew they all knew where Sam was, but they wouldn't tell. Both horses in the corral, and everybody doing the same thing they did every day. It was almost theatrical.

It was strange having a meal at one end of Sam's long dining-room table. His staff to wait on us, and our host absent. His place between us laid but vacant. We hoped he might turn up any minute, but he didn't. No host. We wondered whether that call to war was his way of showing us the door. But we couldn't leave. No way out! No transport.

OCTOBER 12

It is like being aboard ship under sail, but with the captain locked in his cabin and destination unknown. The crew get on with their customary jobs – the herdsman and the dairy-man, the chicken-keeper, the groom and his horses, but not the mechanic. (Now idle, no spare parts.) All cheerful, invari-ably polite, some with more English than others, all going about their business as though everything was normal. We get the feeling this has happened before. Staff seem wholly unconcerned as to the whereabouts of our skipper – mum is the universal word.

A little like being stranded aboard the *Marra* – at least old Hadj didn't go A.W.O.L.

Feeding 20 people and 40 dogs is achieved effortlessly. Each morning a buck of some sort is carried in and butchered. We have not heard a shot fired. We suppose the beast has been caught or trapped in some stealthy way only they know how to do. We are living among all these Africans about whom we know nothing. The tradition of Sam's hospitality rolls on, with us as the beneficiaries. In the evening we receive the best cut of the buck. The rest goes to staff. Bones, gristle, and skin are boiled up, mixed with rice, and the broth fed to the dogs.

You might imagine feeding 40 dogs would be total mayhem, but it all goes off without a growl or a whimper. The mastiffs and ridgebacks get fed first from huge bowls, then on down the line according to size. Anthony Barkus comes near the end. Now that he has become our official personal pet, he is rewarded with scraps under the table.

Another day passed without event. Marooned in paradise. No other word for it. Everything taken care of. Our laundry: dirty and rumpled in the morning, freshly washed and pressed in the evening. Not a chore to do. Besieged by idleness. Thus the only option: to write. We advanced the breakfast hour from 5 a.m. to 8, out on the veranda with majestic Mt. Kenya presiding, elixir air. The great African silence. Yet we were disturbed. We did not enjoy our food. We were taking advantage of our absent host. We concluded that the call to battle was his weird way of scaring us off. If we could leave, we would, but we can't. We questioned the wisdom of walking out and decided against. The Coldstream Guards have dematerialized. Now we miss them. We feel completely isolated. Not a Somali raider in sight.

OCTOBER 13

Horseback riding is the only available mode of transport. I don't like horses or horseback riding, but it appeals to Joe's romantic nature. We are in lion country, with only spears for protection. Assegais. Now what am I supposed to do with my spear – poke it in the beast's eye while he chews my leg off?

We rode out across dry, thorny country – hot, buzzing with locusts, hostile and unpleasant. Weirdly not unlike walking through the Amazonian rainforest: every minute you are expecting some aggressive biting or stinging beast to rear up or jump out. They rarely do; they're more scared of us than we are of them. Nevertheless you stay on red alert, nerves on edge.

By contrast, all around Sam's home is soft, cool, and green. A reliable water supply, fed by a spring up in the hills behind the house, allows his staff to irrigate and sprinkle. Thus his productive vegetable garden – tended by multiple gardeners, men and women, their children – and the colorful flowers, but no lawn.

Some baboons were traveling around. We had been told to avoid them. A pair of ostriches in the distance. We spotted some giraffe browsing. Now this was something special. This was the rare, reticulated (or Rothschild), brightly marked variety, Sam had told us, who found refuge on his acres. They were gigantic and majestically graceful. We trotted toward them. They regarded us from on high, benignly, like superior beings, seemingly friendly but alert. As we closed, they began to move. No trotting or galloping for them, but a fluid canter. Joe led the chase. I deliberately lagged behind, but Joe was fearless. Stones and clods of dirt as big as grapefruit shot past my head. Those animals were huge!

OCTOBER 14, IMPALA FARM

Discovery. I rose early to pee and, half asleep, spotted one of the "boys" carrying a case of beer across the garden. Wide awake, I crept along and spied. He took the beer to one of the outbuildings, known as "the creamery," and tapped on the door. The door opened. The beer went in. The door shut. So that's where our host is hiding: in "the creamery."

OCTOBER 15

To describe accurately the world we are living in, and by that I mean the real world, one that is very close to nature, I must include the event which occurred yesterday.

After our ride out, and as we did each evening, Joe and I were sitting with our cocktails on the veranda, taking in the breathtaking view. The setting sun was turning the snowy peaks of Mt. Kenya from vanilla to strawberry. Maybe raspberry. The silence profound. Except for the occasional honk of birds settling down for the night (the "Austrian" pond had geese on it), the roar of some distant predator, or the pathetic diminishing squeals of some helpless animal being swallowed alive, the African world was moving peacefully toward night.

Sam's dogs lay all around us. Missing their master, craving affection, they followed us everywhere, with Anthony

Barkus in pride of place. We had been advised not to give him scraps at mealtime, which naturally produced a snarling face-off under the table.

Forty dogs: it is hard to describe the many mismatched mongrels among them. One thing they have in common: they are all incredibly hardy and tough, even our Anthony Barkus. They supplement breakfast with rats and whatever vermin dare to venture within a mile of this place. We haven't seen so much as a mouse since we've been here.

So while we were mulling over the mysterious absence of our host, the reason why he was behaving in such a bizarre manner, after that long-distance invitation and all those welcoming and helpful letters along the way, not to mention the months of hard travel it took to get to Kenya, we were presented with a singular, savage, and unforgettable spectacle.

As I had already noted, Sam's lodge faced down over a gently concave plain framed by rocky cliffs left and right, with Mt. Kenya, like an enormous wedding cake (now definitely raspberry), occupying center stage.

We had already spotted, first with the naked eye, then picked out with our binoculars, baboons sitting and moving among the boulders to the right, obviously sentinels, keeping a sharp lookout for their enemy, the leopard.

We saw baboons on our ride out. We had been told what powerful, dangerous, and unpredictable animals they were, and accordingly gave them a wide berth.

Now something was happening – we didn't quite know what. Instead of a few large male baboons keeping watch, there were dozens, all different sizes, maybe hundreds of animals bounding down the rocks, including mothers with babies on their backs. They were heading out across the valley toward the rocky escarpment on the other side. It seemed that a baboon migration was going on.

Joe and I were enthralled by this African spectacle being played out in front of us. There we were, feet up, G. & T.'s in our mitts, being treated to a scene most wildlife cameramen would wait months to capture.

The dogs saw or smelled. It sounded like a pack of horses leaving the veranda. The noise, the yelps, the excitement. All led by our own Anthony Barkus, who was sitting on my lap and had the first top view.

All 40 dogs charged the baboon migration.

The baboon is a large muscular predator with sharp incisors and an appetite for anything that comes his way. Some of our warriors were Yorkshire terriers, or their mongrel equivalents. In minutes it was over – a snarling, barking, screaming scrum of animals killing animals. Then the baboons scattered and fled back to the escarpment. Migration over.

Our team trailed back to the house. Some but not all. Some with their intestines dragging on the ground. They had to be put down. Our own Anthony Barkus was not among them.

Joe and I finished our drinks and headed for the dining room. How much longer were we going to be marooned here? How were we going to leave? This was a devil's paradise: one of the most beautiful places in the world, but with no way out.

Walk? Saddle up and ride out? The telephone never rang. No dial tone. Line dead.

Yesterday's event has made us feel more insecure in this beautiful yet potentially dangerous land we do not understand. Chained to paradise!

*

Anthony Barkus' mangled corpse was brought in, the whole bottom half of his body missing. Ripped in two by a beast ten times his size. What was left we buried in Sam's extensive dog cemetery.

We have time on our hands. Plenty. Too much. I study Swahili. We do a lot of reading. I write home describing our adventures, wondering if these missives will ever reach their destination. Will they make it to the post office in Nanyuki? The diary lends some structure to the amorphous, ambiguous existence we are enduring.

Each day before lunch we knock on the door of the creamery.
"Hey, Sam, come on out!"
"Sam, we miss you!"
"Sam, it's cocktail time. Joe is mixing Ramos gin fizzes!"
"Mint juleps!"
Silence. We've been talking to the door. The whole situation is getting more and more weird.

OCTOBER 16

Eureka! Yesterday at dusk we were out on the veranda, having the usual "sundowner," when we spotted a pair of lights heading up the drive. We reacted with the frantic anticipation of the marooned when a sail appears on the vacant horizon.

We ran out to greet a rugged old-timer, with a full head of snow-white hair, as he stepped from a battered Land Rover.

Will Powys by name. Turned out to be the brother of the Welsh writer, John Cowper Powys. Didn't matter who he was. We were never so glad to see anybody in our lives.

We went back to the veranda. Mt. Kenya: the raspberry hour. Mr. Powys accepted a glass of whiskey in his big brown hands. No ice. We described our predicament. Sam was present but not here; we were the guests of an invisible host. This was his whiskey we were drinking.

Mr. Powys did not seem surprised. He owns a ranch about 20 miles away and is in the habit of dropping by every now and then to check how his neighbor is getting on. Sam, he said, is very lonely.

On one visit, he told us, Sam's house was ablaze with light. Mr. Powys assumed a party must be going on. But no Land Rovers were parked outside. Not another car in sight.

He peeked through the dining-room window. There was Sam, dressed in his Royal Canadian Navy uniform, battle ribbons and all, regaling his guests at the long dinner table. All his silver, polished and shining, was on display. One of his "boys," in full livery, stood behind each of the 12 chairs.

Sam was the only one present. All the other chairs were empty. He was addressing a phantom audience. He had made a huge effort to make his dining room look its best: flowers on the table, staff's immaculate livery, with tarbooshes and a sumptuous feast.

We told Mr. Powys about Sam's invitation to the Ivy Club at Princeton, the long letters, the trip across Africa, and how we came to be stranded in Sam's romantic and comfortable home, with servants galore, excellent food, the magnificent landscape to contemplate or explore. The only thing missing was our host, which made us edgy and uncomfortable. Here we were, indulging in his hospitality, taking advantage of every pleasure his ranch had to offer, but no Sam.

Mr. Powys said we were right not to try to leave. One other marooned and bewildered guest had tried to walk the 30 miles or so to Nanyuki and got lost. Lucky not to have been mauled by lions. With the exception of one shotgun for snakes, he said, Sam's guns had been confiscated by the District Commissioner, because of his alcoholic reputation. With no shooting allowed, the animals had learned by instinct they would be safe on Impala Farm. Game of every sort drifted in. Sam's acres had become a kind of mini game reserve, and therefore potentially unsafe for an unarmed man on foot.

Joe and I looked at each other: no wonder we had Massu and his poison arrows outside our door.

Mr. Powys had no precise explanation for Sam's behavior. Alone and lonely, Sam invited many people to visit. Mr. Powys thought the vanishing acts might have something to do with Sam's past — why he was unmarried, and the circumstances of his acquiring this vast farm in Kenya. It was unusual, he said, for an unmarried man to live alone, miles from his nearest neighbor. Why wasn't he back in Maryland with family and friends, etc.? He said Sam suffered from asthma. Kenya's climate agreed with him, one of the reasons he moved to Africa. To me it seems a long way to come for an asthma cure. He also had English army friends in the area who encouraged him to settle in Kenya. He came here in 1952, at the beginning of the Mau Mau uprising, and probably bought Impala Farm for a song.

Mr. Powys added that as far as he knew there wasn't a Somali cattle raider within 100 miles.

This Mr. Will Powys is a very attractive and impressive gent. About 70 years old and extremely fit. He arrived in Kenya in 1914 to herd sheep. The Welsh know everything about sheep. In those days, he said, there were also herds of rhino. There were more rhino than sheep.

He knocked on the creamery door and called to his neighbor to come out. No answer.

"Grab your toothbrushes, boys, come with me."

Which we gladly did. We ran to our room, threw a few clothes into a bag, and hopped into the Land Rover.

The relief in exiting paradise! Mingled with regret that the whole Impala Farm experience, so eagerly looked forward to, and for so long, had become one big question mark. It seemed that Sam took one look at two young fellow Princetonians, traveling the world and having the time of their lives, and sort of went nuts. Maybe this was what he should have done, would have liked to have done, but didn't. He sat, day after day, in an alcoholic stupor, in the creamery, dreaming of what might have been.

OCTOBER 17

Will Powys lives on this ranch near Timau. Wife absent or deceased (no mention of her). Grown children with farms of their own. This is a tidy working ranch, not glamorous like Impala Farm but, with the master of the house presiding, we feel welcome and at home.

In the afternoon we drove around with Mr. Powys in his Land Rover, opening gates and helping him with various jobs on the farm, mainly repairing fence lines that contain his cattle but have been trampled down by big game.

On the way home we were driving past a hill, an oddly shaped conical hill that stood alone on the vast thorny plain.

Mr. Powys stopped the vehicle.

"I've always wanted to climb that hill," he said, "but back

in the days when I was young enough to do it, we were on horses, and I was always afraid a lion would take my pony while I was up."

"Let's do it," Joe suggested. "Let's do it now. We'll give you a hand."

By pushing and pulling (at 70 he was still strong, but with legs not so strong), we got this pioneer to the summit. He sat on a flat rock for almost an hour, sun going down, taking in the view he had been visualizing all these years. Not just Mt. Kenya, which you see from everywhere, but a huge spread of veldt, invisible from Sam's house. He seemed mighty pleased, and I think we won his heart today on that hill. He certainly won ours.

OCTOBER 18

Another day on the fence lines. Hot, sweaty work. Good to be using the body again, but it confirmed for me that the idea of coffee farming in Peru was never going to be more than a romantic chimera. But Peru was more than coffee. It was a colorful inspiration (I don't think anyone actually believed we would carry it through) which loosened us from the confining limits of family expectations and gave us enough slack to imagine the rest of our lives.

Mr. Powys, alert to everything, spotted a herd of "Tommies" (Thomson's gazelles) on the plain. About 200 or 300 yards distant, wobbly in the heat. He got down the rifle that lay on hooks behind our heads in the Land Rover.

"Do one of you boys want to have a go? My cook does a mighty fine buck fillet."

It was decided I would have a go. When I was about ten, my father gave me a .22 single-shot rifle, which I used to pick off rabbits and squirrels; but I have never before handled a heavy, high-powered, telescopic-sighted weapon, in this case a .318 Rigby. Following Mr. Powys' instructions, I lay on the ground and rested the rifle on the doubled-up gun sleeve. He told me to relax, not to hurry, take a deep breath, let it out, and slowly squeeze, not pull, the trigger when I had the beast in the crosshairs.

I squinted through the scope. The intense heat blurred my vision. I couldn't see a thing. When I finally focussed on a beast, it looked as though it were jumping up and down.

I pulled, not squeezed. I knew I was going to miss. I had no confidence. The gazelle never moved. He didn't even know that someone had shot at him. I must have missed by a mile.

"Give me that gun."

Joe lay down in the dust, legs spread wide, and accepted another slug from our host.

After Princeton he had spent six months in the U.S. Army. The only medal he came home with was for "top marksman."

He squeezed the trigger. Miles away an animal dropped.

"Great shot!"

Mr. Powys was standing on the Land Rover, watching through binoculars.

We ran forward to inspect the kill. All the "Tommies" had scattered but one – a delicate beige and white beast, with a bloodstain on his chest.

"You murderer!" I shouted.

Joe laughed. "Well, you had the first go, my friend, and you missed."

Mr. Powys drove up in the Land Rover.

"That was an excellent shot. Two hundred and fifty yards in this heat. Now we're going to have a fine supper."

OCTOBER 21, QUEENS HOTEL, NAIROBI

Joe lethargic and down with fever, again. This time not low but high. 103°. He was burning up. Mr. Powys drove us to the British military hospital in Nanyuki. The young soldier–doctor listened to his chest and pronounced pneumonia. Double.

I now fear our Kenyan adventure is drawing to a close. So much sooner than expected. Far too soon. Baggage lost or stolen. (We suspect stolen.) *White Nile* broken. Debacle chez Sam. Now pneumonia. Double! It is beginning to look like the end of the line.

From the hospital I went to the Nanyuki P.O. to collect our mail, which included a notice from customs at Nairobi Airport. A package awaited, provenance Munich.

The motorcycle parts. Important to get the machine up and running. We can't go anywhere without her.

I took Joe his letters, left him in a haze of penicillin, caught a military lift to Nairobi, ate and drank dinner, and checked back into Queens.

Just as I was about to switch the light off came a tap on the door. There stood a 16-year-old pixie with ribbons in her hair.

"Did you request room service, sir?"

She spoke excellent English.

I hadn't, actually. I remembered, however, in my semi-inebriated state, asking the doorman if it was too late (11 p.m.) for a nightcap to be brought to my room. I think he winked at me.

My "nightcap" went by the name of Sheila. It was a bit disappointing when she took off the wig with the pretty ribbons sewn into it. Even more when she unfastened her bra. Her boobs, which at the door had revealed exceptional cleavage for one so young, dropped by a couple of inches. Stretch marks indicated she was the mother of a family. I revised her age upwards: 18, maybe 20. The price was $10, plus another 10 for "Willie" at the door.

I went to collect the machine on "Motorbike Street," where capable Indian mechanics repair every make of English bike.

The economies of East Africa are controlled by Indians. They came over years ago to work on the railroads and never went home. Their families followed. Now they have a stranglehold on the money. All of it. Every shop, store, garage, bank, and money-lending establishment in Uganda and Kenya is run by Indians. They have the jobs the Africans want. And they treat the Africans badly – worse than anyone else. One step up on the ladder, they crush the hand on the rung below. Wearing turbans, they stick together. They keep prices high and make you haggle over a stick of gum.

OCTOBER 22

I putt-putted the still ailing machine to the airport. What awaited me was not a parcel but a wooden crate. BMW Munich had sent a brand-new engine! Free of charge! Not even a postage stamp! I had to hire a truck to carry it to Nairobi. A crowd of mechanics gathered on Motorbike Street to admire the beautiful silver engine, with its horizontally opposed cylinders (which nobody had ever seen before). As the wooden packaging was stripped away, out emerged a sleek, shiny machine flown in from planet Mars.

I left Ali to put her back together again and, defying Sam's warning, hitch-hiked back to Nanyuki.

Joe's condition has improved but he is not out of the woods, not yet. News of the arrival of the new engine lifted his spirits.

"Johnny, that fellow we bought the motorcycle from in Munich must remember us."

His voice was alarmingly weak. I thought, holy shit, he's got to get well! Everything is going wrong for us in Kenya.

So much has happened since our trip to Germany in May. Buying the machine within an hour of getting off the train in Munich seems eons ago.

We held a strategy session. We have left some clothes at Sam's. The clothes don't matter but our passports and binoculars are in the same bag.

Mr. Powys turned up with some "buck broth" for the patient. He drove me to Impala Farm, where the river stopped us. With the recent heavy rains, what had been a trickle a week ago has become a heavy torrent. He was unable to get the Land Rover across. There was no choice but to wade in and swim for it. Sam had warned us of crocodiles lurking. Mr. Powys doubted they would be active in such a current. The croc is a stealthy predator and likes still water. Nevertheless, he got down the Rigby, loaded up, and kept a lookout while I splashed to the other side. I waved goodbye to this remarkable man and, soaking wet, walked the last two miles to Sam's house.

OCTOBER 23, IMPALA FARM

Still no Sam! I can hardly believe it. We have been away over a week and he is still in the creamery. The ranch as beautiful as ever. The staff and dogs as welcoming. But no Sam. And no Anthony Barkus.

Joe and I were both hoping that by this time Sam would be back in circulation. Back to normal. To whatever he was before. We are prepared to let bygones be bygones. Make a fresh start and start the visit all over again. Make his house our headquarters/hotel, and come and go as we please, as he had repeatedly proposed in his letters. But no. What do we do now? The situation is bewildering. He seems to have become allergic the moment he clapped eyes on us. Maybe he hadn't anticipated the impact of two young men traveling the world would have upon his lonely, unfulfilled dreams.

Another blow. The binoculars are missing. The beautiful, lightweight, powerful Zeiss binoculars, which I bought in Munich the same day as the machine and which, like the machine, have been with us the whole way, and which have come in incredibly handy spotting game – crocodiles, buffalo, hippos, elephant, baboons, giraffe – are gone.

With everything else going wrong at Impala Farm, I didn't complain. Massu was a hunter; maybe he took them. He is welcome to them. We have accepted so much hospitality, pointing fingers now would be out of place. I accepted the loss in silence and sadness. Sadness, mostly, for the way this trip is teetering toward conclusion. What we had expected to be the high point, indeed the whole point, has turned out to be the low point. We had hoped to spend several months exploring this vast and beautiful continent, not only the game parks but Mombasa and the coast, maybe travel south into Tanganyika and beyond, always returning to Impala Farm for R and R. This was all Sam's idea. His absence has thrown a wet blanket over the whole project.

Plus, Joe's health has put a damper on things. In that hospital room in Nanyuki, we just about decided, unless I found a new Sam, to call the rest of the trip off. Now with the binoculars gone it looks like our days in Africa are numbered. Little things like this can tip the scales.

OCTOBER 25

I was looking out the window at an airplane parked on the lawn.

Gilford Powys is about my age, maybe a few years older, but bigger, stronger, and a whole lot tougher. He lives alone, womanless, on his numberless acres. He rescued me from Sam's by prearrangement with his father. Father and son communicated by radio across the empty spaces. The plan is for me to spend a few days with him, helping on the farm, as there is no big hurry to return to Nanyuki. Joe is on the mend, but needs more time to recover. Sam's continued absence is having an evolving impact on this trip. I don't expect to see our host again. Obviously he doesn't want to see us. As soon as Joe is well enough to travel, and the machine repaired, I imagine we'll start making plans to leave Africa.

Unless something turns up.

Neither of us looks forward to returning to Europe with winter coming on, with less money, with no plans, and far fewer hopes than before.

My asthma has begun to act up. Maybe due to the stress of everything going wrong. I pulled my shorts back, dropped the syringe into the top of my thigh, and waited for the adrenalin rush.

Gilford rose at 3 a.m. and had done half a day's work before I got out of bed. He shot three buck, two standing up in the front yard, the third out the window of the Land Rover. He gave two to "the boys," and we feasted on the other. On his shelves are his famous uncle's books; not one has been opened. Tomorrow we are going flying.

OCTOBER 26

The plane parked outside the house was a lemon-yellow Piper Cub, the exact same model as the one I took lessons in, soloed in, and got my license in at the Pluckemin Airport back in New Jersey, when I was still at Princeton. Gilford's has soft fat tires for landing and taking off over rough ground.

Gilford piloted the aircraft off the ground (he knew where the "gophers" made their holes) before handing the controls over to me. I sat up front in the narrow cockpit. He told me to head ESE at 110°.

The purpose of this trip was buffalo. He was leaning out the window with binoculars – which he said was very difficult, awkward, and dangerous to do, with one hand on the stick – understatement of the year – spying out for beasts. This guy knows no fear. With the window wide open, oppressive engine noise.

He told me to take it up to 5,000'. I gunned the RPMs, eased back on the stick, and tried to maintain airspeed. There was a lot of mountain out there. Also cloud. Visibility not good. I was getting nervous because I didn't know the lay of the land. I am used to rolling N.J. farmland, not a snow-capped mountain in Africa. But hunter Gilford was obsessed with spotting his beasts.

A cloud bank loomed ahead. I yelled at Gilford: "You take over! I don't know my way around!" He dropped the binocs and grabbed the stick. Suddenly we were in a total white-out, with a 17,000' wall in front of us.

He shouted. "I'm no good at maths! What's the opposite of 120°?"

A cold hand gripped my heart. My mind went blank. Holy shit. What was he talking about? The penny dropped. He's talking about compass readings!

(You have to add or subtract 180° from your compass reading before you do a mid-air U-turn and head back toward where you came from.)

"300°!"

He peeled into such a tight turn I practically pitched out the window. Through the mist I caught a glimpse of green forest a few hundred feet below. Another minute and we would have flown straight into it.

He found clear air. Heart pumping, I took over again.

Gilford back with the binocs. I don't think he ever went to flying school. He must have learned by the seat of his pants. Didn't bother with a seat belt. Maybe that's the best way out here.

He spotted his beasts. How, in that deep forest? To me they looked like black beetles moving through the heavy green brush that coats the lower slopes of Mt. Kenya.

He radioed a message in Swahili. He was fluent.

Back on the grass strip, avoiding the gopher holes. No chocks under wheels. No flying report. No logbook. We ran to the Land Rover and raced up the flanks of Mt. Kenya. Gilford knew the way, better than he knew it by air. We reached the end of the track. Thick jungle. Meadows in between. He pulled a heavy rifle from the rack and like Tarzan ran off into the woods.

"Follow me!"

That was the last I saw of him for a couple of hours.

He vanished into the forest. After eight years on the ice rink, I thought I was in pretty good shape, but nothing compared to this monument.

I ran, I walked, I rested on a log and smoked a cigarette; I trotted and sometimes crawled through dense underbrush. There was a trail of sorts. I followed the buffalo tracks in the mud, half expecting one of them to show himself at any minute.

After about two or three miles, completely lost, I heard a gunshot up ahead. And there was my host, sitting on top of a black beast, handing out cigarettes. He was surrounded by African beaters, trackers, tree-climbers. His whole team was there.

The long walk back to the Land Rover. We drove to the Mt. Kenya Safari Club and had cocktails with William Holden. All in a day's work.

OCTOBER 28, NAIROBI

Joe healing but pale, peaked. Still far from his old self. Like Joe, the *White Nile* is running better but not completely cured. Photo with machine and interview in the *East African Standard*. This looks like the end of the road, but we are not ready to let go of Africa – not quite yet.

OCTOBER 30, MOMBASA

We hitch-hiked down to the coast (machine still undergoing repairs) and joined the East African Seamen's Union. You have to, if you want to find work on a ship in Mombasa harbor. We have our membership cards, with photographs and fingerprints. We plan to hire a launch to take us around to the freighters lying out there, hopefully to find a job on one traveling to the Orient.

We have actually done this before, on our first trip to Peru. With the coffee idea fading, we weren't ready to go home, we wanted to prolong the adventure. So we hired a boat in Lima's port, Callao, to ferry us to the steamers lying in the harbor to find working passage to the Orient.

Now we are trying to get to Asia again, this time from another direction: from across the Indian, not the Pacific Ocean; not from the west coast of South America but the east coast of Africa, from the opposite side of the world. If luck fails us, as it did in Callao, we plan to thumb a lift back to Nairobi, crate up the machine and mail her to Paris, which we've decided will be our next destination.

NOVEMBER 11, ORLY AIRPORT FREIGHT TERMINAL, PARIS

It was like a hectic search for a dear friend in a huge, unfamiliar hospital. She may have been injured in transit, broken loose from her moorings (which we had so carefully supervised in Nairobi) inside the crate, have been lying on her side, or upside down hemorrhaging oil.

I had the bill of lading with a number on it, the key in my pocket. It has taken her only a week to get here. Very few people about, because it is Armistice Day.

After several detours among thousands of wooden boxes with labels from all over the world, we found her. With a borrowed crowbar we levered off the planks. There she was — clean, intact, and untouched. The Kenyan packers had done a fine job.

Tires low. We pushed her to the first filling station, pumped them up, and gassed up. I inserted the key. One kick and a nostalgic growl from Africa. We hopped on and headed off through the frigid streets of Paris.

But where to next?

The most important experiences are not those you look for, but those that look for you.

ANDRÉ GIDE

*   *   *

EPILOGUE

Paris was cold, gray, wet, crowded, and, compared with what we had been used to paying in Africa, scarily expensive. After several failures we found a room at the Hôtel Lisbonne, at the top of rue de Vaugirard, between the Odéon Théâtre and rue Monsieur-le-Prince. No central heating to speak of, not much hot water, a shared toilet on another floor, but somehow cozy and welcoming. We lived in cafés, bars, restaurants, movie theaters – anywhere where it was warm. We took our meals at one of a nest of cheap restaurants on rue de la Harpe.

As in Rome, we scanned the classified columns of the *Herald Tribune*, looking for jobs to keep us going. Joe struck first: a post teaching English at a lycée in Grignon, near Versailles. The pay wasn't much, but included room and board, and was less than an hour by train to Paris.

I landed a job running a school for the U.S. Army in a village called Étain, near Verdun, in eastern France. It was 300 km from Paris, but the pay compensated: $500 per month.

My mother had sent over a suitcase of winter clothes. Even so, with sheepskin jacket, heavy sweater, scarf, ski gloves, and hat, the three-hour drive on the *White Nile* was an ordeal. Meaux, Châlons-sur-Marne, Verdun, and Étain with the icy rain in my face: every hour or so I had to stop at a roadside café for hot tea laced with double rum to chase the chill from my bones.

In Étain I found lodging at 5, rue du Pont with Mme. Xardel, an amiable widow who had seen the armies of two world wars march past her door. Each morning I put on a coat and tie and motored to Caserne Sidi Brahim, a French military base that had been converted to a U.S. Army transport and logistics center. The schoolmaster arriving by motorcycle made me a kind of instant celebrity among the soldiers. My job was to teach 50-year-old black sergeants the basics of English grammar. My classroom was the movie theater, my office the space behind the movie screen.

It was a long, lonely, dreadfully cold winter. In the afternoons after work I tramped the trenches of the *déboisé* Verdun battlefield, where the earth had been so churned up by shellfire that no tree would ever grow again. I visited the forts of Douaumont and Hardoumont, flattened by German artillery, and "*La Tranchée des Baïonnettes.*" That bleak battlefield, where more than half a million men my age had perished, left a deep impression.

Each weekend I motored to Paris to join Joe at the Lisbonne, or, if there was snow on the road, I trained from Verdun, changing at Châlons and arriving at La Gare de l'Est, whence millions of young men had departed for the front, never to return.

To be with Joe in Paris was inspiring. Our friendship was the rock we both stood on. With the present dismal and the future bleak, we spent hours in bars weighing up options. We talked about going to Brazil, but that would be backtracking. And of course our families were urging us to give up this crazy adventure, come home, and get serious.

The fact that I picked up a $500 paycheck at the end of each month kept me optimistic. This was more money than I was used to. The dollar still went a long way in France. It was satisfying to be solvent. I had PX privileges, meaning a bottle of Jack Daniels could be had for $3.

My dad visited, and it was wonderful to have him there. At 63, it was his first trip outside the U.S. We had not met this way before – more like man to man than father and son. I was proud to be his son and hoped he would be proud of me one day.

Upon tasting Pernod for the first time: "It will never be a popular drink."

Upon viewing a Deux Chevaux: "It looks like a car made in someone's backyard."

He sat in on my classes, listening to me teach my sergeants how to read and write:

"Son, you have the most challenging job of anyone I know."

I took time off work, rented a VW Beetle, and we visited the cathedrals of Reims, Chartres, and Notre-Dame. At first I was afraid we wouldn't have much to say; but then I realized we shared large areas of common accord. Never had I felt a blood relationship more strongly. I wondered why. Maybe the trip across Africa had opened my eyes; maybe the truth comes out abroad.

My father was a true southern gentleman. He rarely talked about himself, and never complained. He suffered terribly from the loss of his family, but he carried his pain with dignity and only said:

"It is a lonely life."

Mme. Xardel had a weakness for Verlaine. She was always repeating:

Voici des fruits, des fleurs, des feuilles et des branches
Et puis voici mon cœur qui ne bat que pour vous.

While I was at the base she and my father sipped tea and chatted. They were both about the same age. Mme. Xardel was a widow and my father divorced. Neither spoke a word of the other's language, but they seemed to get on famously.

I employed an attractive, intelligent, well-educated (Bryn Mawr College) wife of an officer to teach English to a handful of soldiers who had actually graduated from high school. Some G.I.s expressed a desire to learn French. I hired Monique not for her brains, but for her award-winning chest. French classroom enrollment doubled. By parsing sentences on the blackboard I was making headway with my sergeants. The construction of our language became clearer to them. The base commander congratulated me on starting up a "cultural center" in the movie theater.

Monique was 19 but had not yet passed her driving test. During the interview she said her mother could drop her off at the base, but she needed a lift home after class. I neglected to say it would be by motorcycle.

We left Caserne Sidi Brahim with the *White Nile* purring between our legs.

There are four steps to seducing a girl on a motorcycle.

STEP 1: You stop at the first bar for a couple of beers.

STEP 2: You gun the machine from the first stoplight. You rocket ahead. Your startled passenger screams and hangs on for dear life.

STEP 3: You drive like a maniac, leaning into curves to scare your passenger, who now clings to you like a limpet. You can feel her boobs pressing against your back.

STEP 4: You have a liberal landlady who doesn't mind whom you bring home, your father or your motorcycle mate, because she's lonely and enjoys company and a bit of mischief.

What sustained me through those long winter months was my diary. Gide said that few of his friends remained true to their youth. Almost all compromised, which they called "learning from life." His *Journals* encouraged me to keep on jotting down small and insignificant entries, usually while dining alone, as I did each night at La Sirène, Étain's only restaurant. As these entries began to add up, I noted my determination to become a writer. But of what? Essays? Novels? Short stories? I had no idea.

Spring came at last. Once more it became a joy to jump on the machine. I visited Sedan, Metz, and Nancy, and explored the Maginot Line. My sergeants passed their exams. We had a booze-up in a local bar. They could look forward to promotion and pay raises.

In Paris Joe had run into Pauline Badham from Birmingham, Alabama. Her brother, J.T., had been his best friend at Princeton. Pauline was married to Joe Pinto, who had gone to the Lawrenceville School and Yale; but he came from a prominent Moroccan Jewish family and had grown up in Casablanca and Tangier, where his family ran a successful sugar and tea business.

Every weekend we were invited to their beautiful apartment at 59, boulevard Lannes, where we downed dry Martinis and listened to Joe talk about Morocco. If we missed Africa so much, he asked, why didn't we go to Tangier?

The idea was appealing. We had heard good things about Morocco. But what would we do when we got there? How would we support ourselves in Morocco? It turned out that Joe's father, Jacques, had been one of the founders of the American School of Tangier. We wrote the school and filled out forms. Our teaching experience in France came in handy. The Pintos recommended us, and we were offered jobs in Morocco! On July 2, 1962, we hopped aboard the *White Nile* and, for the second time in less than a year, set off for Africa.

The plan was to spend a year in Morocco. Like in Lerici, we had no idea what to expect. I ended up staying 17. It was that good. In Tangier I became a writer. It was where I met and married Ellen Ann Ragsdale, a world traveler from Little Rock, Arkansas. Joe was my best man. Ellen Ann and I moved to England to raise our family. Joe became the headmaster of the American School of Tangier; he stayed in Morocco the rest of his life.

FORTHCOMING FROM TAURIS PARKE PAPERBACKS

JOHN HOPKINS
The Tangier Diaries

In this cult book Hopkins records the glamour, mystery and exoticism of Tangier in the '60s that was populated by a dazzling mixture of writers, painters, socialites, eccentrics and aristocrats – from William Burroughs and Paul Bowles to Rudolf Nureyev and The Rolling Stones.

———

'It's a beautiful work and I am only sorry that it's not longer. I'd be exceedingly proud to have written it.'
PAUL BOWLES

'Every page drips with memories.'
WILLIAM BURROUGHS

ISBN 978 1 78076 845 8   eISBN 978 0 85773 664 2

FORTHCOMING FROM TAURIS PARKE PAPERBACKS

JOHN HOPKINS

The South American Diaries

By bus, train and dugout canoe, Hopkins
embarks on a haphazard, nomadic and
life-changing journey from Mexico City
to the heart of South America.

'A year in which writer's block turns a novel-
ist into an incomparable diarist.'

ELLE

'One of his best books. Everything is there, the sub-
tlety of his vision, the bitter lucidity, his deep interest in other people and his own yearnings.'

L'ARGUS DE LA PRESSE

ISBN 978 1 78076 825 0   eISBN 978 0 85773 665 9